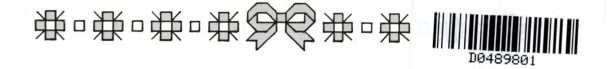

PICTURE IT
in
CROSS STITCH

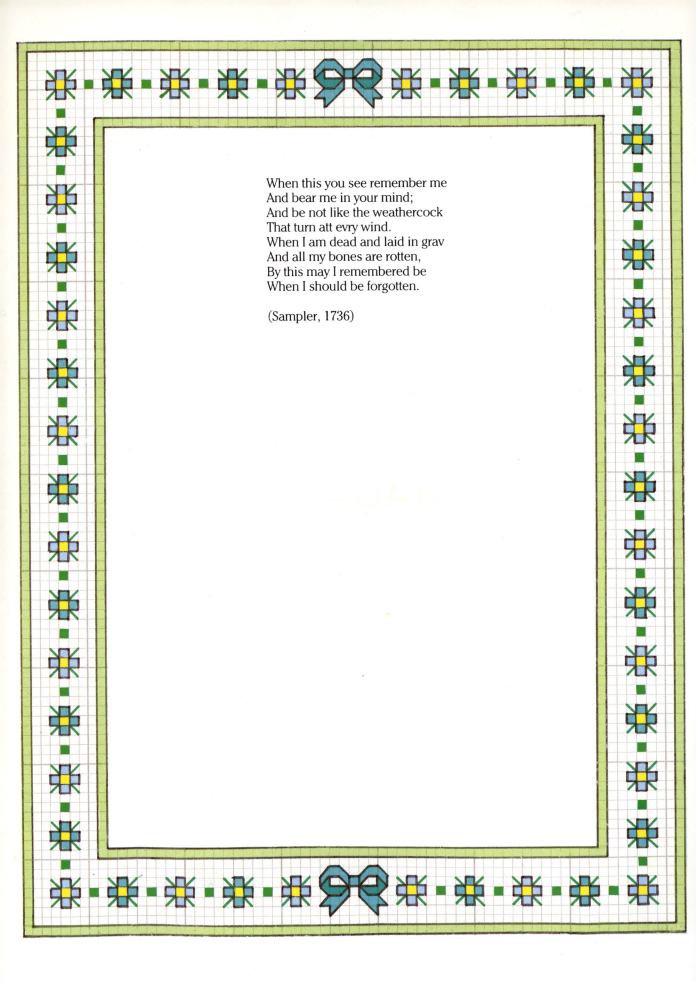

When this you see remember me
And bear me in your mind;
And be not like the weathercock
That turn att evry wind.
When I am dead and laid in grav
And all my bones are rotten,
By this may I remembered be
When I should be forgotten.

(Sampler, 1736)

PICTURE IT
in
CROSS STITCH

Jo Verso

with charts and line illustrations by the author

A David & Charles Craft Book

This book is dedicated to the memory of my grandfather, Hopkin Harries, bespoke tailor, who taught me to thread my first needle at Cloth Hall, Betws, Wales

I would like to thank Helen Fairfield for her encouragement, without which this book might not yet have been written, and Sylvia Morgan who embroidered 'Gather Ye Rosebuds,', 'The Royal Wedding', and the Verso Family Tree with such patience and expertise. My thanks also to the following people who gave permission to publish work in their possession: Mr and Mrs E. A. W. Verso, Mr and Mrs J. Pinnix, Mr and Mrs A. Moore, Mr and Mrs K. Reaves, Mr J. Edwards, Mrs L. Sheen, Mr P. Jacques and Ms S. Read.

British Library Cataloguing in Publication Data
Verso, Jo
  Picture it in cross stitch.
  1. Embroidery, Cross stitch – Patterns
  I. Title
  746.44

ISBN 0-7153-9098-8 H/B
ISBN 0-7153-9485-1 P/B

© text Jo Verso 1988
© line illustrations and charts Jo Verso 1988
© colour photographs Jo Verso and David & Charles 1988
First published 1988
First published in paperback 1991
Reprinted 1991 (3 times)
Reprinted 1992 (twice), 1993 (twice)

Phototypeset by ABM Typographics Limited Hull
and printed in Italy
by LEGO SpA, Vicenza
for David & Charles
Brunel House Newton Abbot Devon

Contents

Introduction

Ten years ago, shortly before the birth of my second daughter, the last few stitches were completed in a patchwork bedspread which had been four years in the making. Standing back to view the result it was obvious that the finishing touch to the room would be an old-fashioned cross-stitch sampler to hang on the wall over the bed. The search for such a sampler led to an absorbing hobby, a new job, and eventually to the writing of this book.

My hunt for a sampler led me first to the local antique shops. Here it became obvious that because samplers were embroidered onto linen, using many coloured threads, they have proved to be decorative and durable documents. Equally their survival is due to the personal nature of these documents incorporating, as they do, details of family life among their borders and alphabets. This personal quality has saved many samplers from being discarded or disposed of for sale, so the few that find their way into antique shops are collectors' items and command high prices beyond my pocket. Reluctantly the decision was made to stitch my own sampler.

The next port of call was the local needlecraft shop to buy a kit. Having embroidered nothing more than a tray-cloth or two at school, it was a relief to see that the main stitch used was cross stitch, one of the easiest stitches to produce with good results. The disappointment was that the kits offered little scope for personalisation other than a few names and dates. What had so appealed about the old samplers was the glimpse they gave into life as it was lived at the time they were sewn. The idea of leaving a picture of my own life to future generations of my family was beginning to appeal to me.

If the decision to stitch my own sampler was taken reluctantly, the prospect of designing it as well was even more daunting. My final destination was the local stationers where a stock of graph paper was bought. Not being an artist, consolation was taken from the observation that cross-stitch patterns tend to be more stylised than naturalistic and there were pattern books from which motifs could be copied. By selectively choosing many bits and pieces out of several books, and making generous use of an eraser, my own design was produced. The result hangs to this day over the bed, complete with all its beginner's mistakes. Along with the traditional border, alphabet, numbers and motifs it portrays my own house, the cat and my family, including the baby, who by the time of sewing had arrived and was represented in her pram. Also included was a motto of my own choice, and all this was sewn in a colour scheme to match the bedspread that had given rise to the whole undertaking. The biggest surprise was that what had appeared at first to be a daunting chore, turned out to be immensely enjoyable, and the satisfaction derived from stitching my own family proved to be addictive.

Since these early beginnings many samplers, pictures, cards and other documents have been produced both for my own family and for friends. This, in turn, led to invitations to teach others how to put together their own designs. Hopefully these will be of interest not only to future generations of our families, but also to needleworkers and social historians as well. To help you to make your own statement in cross-stitch embroidery, this book contains all the patterns that my students have asked me to produce over the years and which cannot easily be found in existing cross-stitch pattern books, together with suggestions and instructions for putting them together to make uniquely personal and contemporary designs. Very few of the patterns will be sewn straight off the page without any alteration. Most are designed as a basic pattern, a starting point, and instructions are given so that you can make changes to suit your circumstances. Some of the photographs show how the basic pattern has already been adapted; all you have to do is study the differences and make your own personal changes according to your taste and the instructions.

Many of the charts in this book are produced in colour to give a good idea of how the embroidery will look when it is finished. The black and white charts have been shaded, not as any indication of the colour which should be used, but merely to give the designs depth and definition on the page. Colour them according to your personal choice, or follow the colours in the embroidered examples.

Just as knitting patterns advise you to check your tension before starting a pattern, or a good result cannot be guaranteed, so the first four chapters should be read carefully by beginners before a project is started. At the end of the book there is a section called Pattern Library with extra patterns which can be taken and added to the basic ones. Hopefully you will find here many symbols applicable to your life or to that of your friends, and you will be inspired to try your hand at designing. Many people react with terror at the idea of having to draw, but most of the work in this book requires simple copying, and mistakes made in copying are easily erased. If you are hesitant, remember that nobody has to see your first efforts and you have nothing to lose by 'having a go'. Also, as this is your statement, if it looks right to you, then it is right. In these days of mass production handmade embroidery is to be prized, and even more so if it tells a story and reflects its maker's personality.

Plate 1 My first effort

ABCDEFGHIJKLMNOPQRSTUVW
XYZ
1234567
89101112
There Is No
Place Like Home
WELCOME TO YOUR NEW HOME

1 Preparing to Design

To produce your own, personalised cross-stitch picture, be it a greetings card or a sampler, you will need a chart to serve as a pattern from which you will work the stitches. Charts in this book are intended to be used as a basis to which you will add your own details. To adapt a chart thus, you will need to copy and make changes to the basic charts, and you should therefore equip yourself with some drawing materials. These are readily available and most can be borrowed from any schoolchild.

GRAPH PAPER

Cross-stitch patterns are drawn onto graph paper and are then translated into stitches by counting the squares on the chart and translating each filled square into one full cross stitch on the fabric (Fig 1). Graph paper is available at good stationers and can be bought as separate sheets, by the roll, or in pads of sheets. Small sheets can be glued together to form larger ones, taking care to line up the squares accurately at the join. Most people find that the best graph paper for this work is one which has ten squares to 1in (2.5cm). The squares are not so small that you strain your eyes whilst you are drawing on them, nor so large that the finished chart is unwieldy to use as a pattern when sewing. You will need a sheet large enough for your finished design, called a master sheet, and spare graph paper onto which you will draw the many different 'ingredients' of your design, which could be motifs, symbols, figures, lettering etc. There is a sheet of graph paper with ten squares to 1in (2.5cm) on page 9 to get you started.

Fig 1 One full square on the chart becomes one full cross stitch on the fabric

PENCILS, CRAYONS AND SCISSORS

Lead pencil
Not all pencils are a pleasure to use, so experiment with a few until you find one which suits you. Choose one with a lead which is soft enough to erase easily, but not so soft that it smudges. Try an HB or a B. A propelling pencil has the advantage that it does not need frequent sharpening.

Pencil sharpener
The pencil must not be blunt; a sharp line is important when drawing on the graph paper to produce an accurate pattern. A craft knife is an excellent choice for sharpening, especially for crayons which persist in breaking in an ordinary sharpener.

Eraser
Use a good quality eraser. The type which slips onto the end of a pencil ensures that your eraser is always to hand when it is needed. Unless you are a Leonardo da Vinci or can copy effortlessly and accurately, you are going to make mistakes and the eraser will be outworn long before the pencil.

Coloured crayons
If you colour in your chart with the approximate colours you intend to use when you come to sew the design, you will have a fair indication of how the finished result will look before you have sewn a single stitch. A colour chart is easier to follow at the sewing stage than a black and white chart which uses key symbols to indicate colour changes. However, no range of coloured crayons can accurately match the enormous number of coloured threads that are available, so be content to give an indication of the colour to be used rather than an accurate guide. A packet of children's crayons, containing about a dozen colours, should be sufficient. More subtle decisions about colour can be made later when the threads are chosen.

Scissors
Paper-cutting scissors are needed to cut out your ingredients for arrangement on the master sheet. Do not be tempted to use your sharp embroidery scissors as you will blunt them if you use them to cut paper.

ADHESIVE
You will need adhesive to fix your ingredients to the master sheet once you have decided on their final position. Adhesive is also needed to stick small sheets of

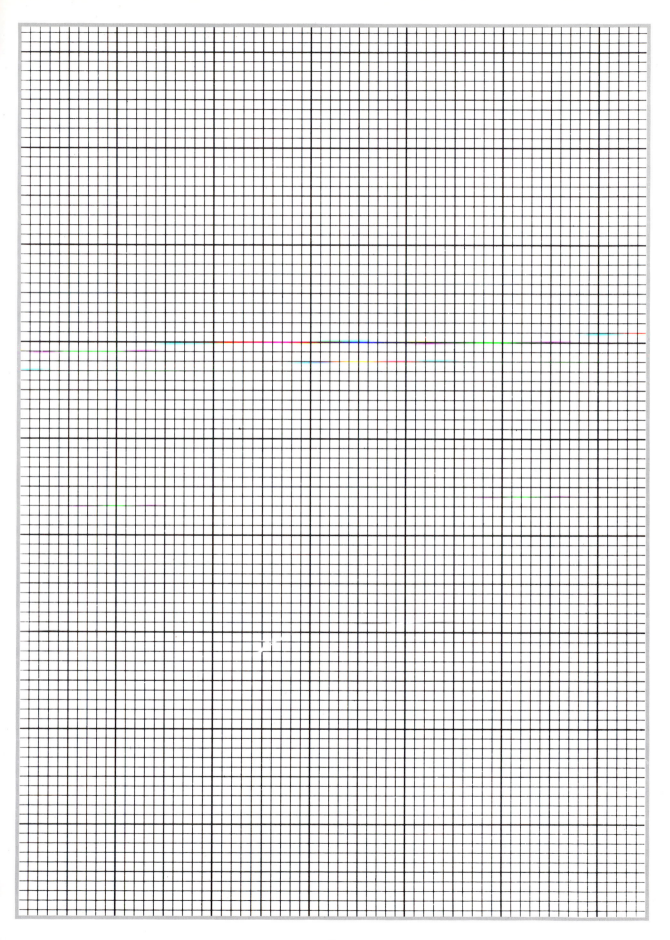

graph paper together to make larger ones. Sticky tape is not suitable. Use an adhesive which will not wet and distort the paper, making it difficult to align the squares on the graph paper. If you are the decisive type and trust your own judgement you can use a glue which, once applied, does not allow for re-positioning. A solid glue which comes in stick form is ideal. If you use cow gum you can change your mind, even weeks later, over the positioning of a design. Once dry, you can (with care) peel the paper off without tearing or marking the master sheet; with another application of gum you can try again. There is also an aerosol adhesive used for mounting photographs and art work; this has the advantage that one spray allows you to peel and re-stick several times before another application is necessary.

TRACING PAPER

If you are unable to find the design you require, ready charted in a book for you to copy, do not be daunted at the prospect of having to produce your own. Tracing paper comes to the rescue of everyone who feels he is no good at drawing. Anything which you cannot draw can be traced from a book, or other source, and can be transferred to the graph paper where it is squared-up to produce an embroidery pattern (see Chapter 2). Greaseproof paper will do at a pinch, but real tracing paper, available at good stationers, is superior in every respect. Graphed tracing paper is tracing paper with the graph grid printed onto it, and is available in book form from good stationers and needlework shops. This graphed tracing paper is laid over the design which is traced onto the squares (Fig 2), ready for squaring-up.

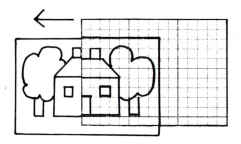

Fig 2 Graphed tracing paper is laid over an illustration

Some modern photocopiers can copy a sheet of graph paper onto transparent acetate sheets, such as are used in overhead projectors. This transparent sheet can then be laid over an illustration and the pattern is at once clearly visible, in colour, through the grid on the sheet. It can then be copied straight onto graph paper.

A LIGHT SOURCE

Tracing is made easier if a light is placed behind the work in progress. The most readily available source of light during daylight hours is a window, and this is adequate for most needs. The work to be traced is positioned behind the tracing paper and is then held up against the glass. However, holding this position for any length of time is guaranteed to make your arms ache. If you

become addicted to this work and are going to do a lot of tracing, you might consider allowing yourself the luxury of a light box (Fig 3).

The Verso version of a light box started life as an old biscuit tin. A central hole for the flex was made in the base of the tin which was then screwed onto a wooden base. A channel was carved in this base to house the flex, and the bulb holder was screwed in place inside the tin. For safety reasons three-core cable must be used, with the earth connected to the biscuit tin. A sheet of clear perspex was placed over the top to provide a surface on which to work. Ventilation, to stop over-heating, was provided by raising the perspex on two side pieces of wood, screwed to two sides of the tin; this allows air to circulate between the perspex and the small, round 40-watt bulb. The work to be traced is placed on the perspex surface, the bulb is switched on and the tracing can then be made.

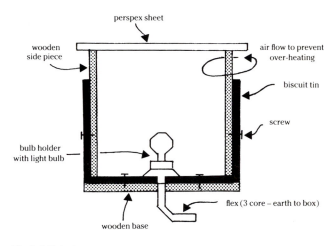

Fig 3 A light box

SOURCES OF DESIGN MATERIAL

Throughout this book you will find patterns which may be suitable for the design you want to create. There are many other cross-stitch pattern books on the market, in which you may find just the designs you want, or you may be able to put together your own chart using a pattern from one book together with patterns from others. Some of the photographs in this book show designs put together in this way to make a more personal picture for the recipient. If you cannot find what you want in an existing pattern book, you may find something which you can adapt and alter to produce the design you want. If all else fails, you will have to make your own design. If you doubt your ability to draw, resort to tracing paper and find pictures to trace of those things you want to depict. An invaluable source of material is your local library, particularly the children's section. Illustrations in children's reference books tend to be simplified line drawings which automatically make easier your task of tracing and squaring-up. Books for babies are particularly good for simplified shapes of animals and everyday objects.

If you are working on a design of your house, you will find it useful to work from a photograph of it. If you do not have access to a camera, you will need a rough sketch. If

Plate 2 Wedding sampler (sources, page 127)

you want to depict a building which is a local landmark you may be able to work from a postcard. Wedding photographs are useful if you want the details of the church, and the appearance of the participants, to be accurate in a wedding design. Reference books and catalogues can usually be relied on to produce a picture of whatever it is you feel unable to draw. At the end of this book there is a Pattern Library and suggestions of other publications which are rich sources of design material.

2 Designing the Chart

Whether you are designing a large picture or a small decorated initial, first make a list of everything you want to include in your design. Each item can then be drawn out onto separate pieces of graph paper. When all the items on the list have been drawn, trim away the excess graph paper around them, ready to arrange them on to a large master sheet of graph paper. This allows you to try many different layouts of your ingredients before deciding on the most pleasing, and saves the irritation of erasing and re-drawing.

DRAWING YOUR ILLUSTRATION

Copying directly onto graph paper
If the items on your list can be found in existing pattern books and you are happy that they do not need to be changed in any way, they can simply be copied directly from the book onto your graph paper. Take care to copy accurately. If the pattern is printed using key symbols to denote colour changes, you may find it easier to colour your chart in with crayons, then, when you come to sew it, you will see at a glance which colour you should be using.

If the pattern in the book needs a change or two of detail to make it more suitable, copy it out as before and erase those areas you want to change. Add the new details you require (see Fig 61).

Tracing an illustration onto graph paper
If the items on your list cannot be found ready charted, you will have to make your own chart, but if you are not artistic there is no need to panic; anything which you feel you cannot draw can be traced from books or other sources. Trace the illustration onto tracing paper, then transfer it onto graph paper. If you choose to use graphed tracing paper, line up as many vertical and horizontal lines as possible before you start to trace your illustration; this will make the job of squaring-up easier. Frequently the illustration of the object you wish to include in your embroidery will be the wrong size for your purposes, so before you trace it on to the graph paper it will need to be reduced or enlarged as the case might be.

Reducing and enlarging
Some modern photocopiers can, by repeated operations, reduce or enlarge an illustration to almost any size required. If you do not have access to a suitable photocopier, take your illustration to your local High Street printer where a copy of the illustration, reduced or enlarged to the size you require, can be obtained at minimal cost. Your illustration can now be traced onto the graph paper ready to be squared-up into a pattern.

SQUARING-UP
Whether you have drawn your illustration directly onto the graph paper or have used tracing paper, it will now need squaring-up to turn it into a pattern for cross-stitch embroidery. At this stage you will probably have a drawing with flowing, curved lines (Fig 4), but in a cross-stitch pattern one full square is translated into one full cross stitch, so all curves must be eliminated leaving only complete squares.

Take your pencil and draw over the lines of your illustration on the graph paper. Follow the original drawing as closely as possible, but never let the pencil stray away from the graph lines. Where the original line starts to climb upwards, bring the pencil line up one square; when it dips, come down one square. Follow the original line all the way round the design; your original flowing shape will now look more angular (Fig 5). Erase the

Fig 4 A drawing is made or traced onto graph paper (left)
Fig 5 The drawing is squared-up (centre)
Fig 6 The finished chart (right)

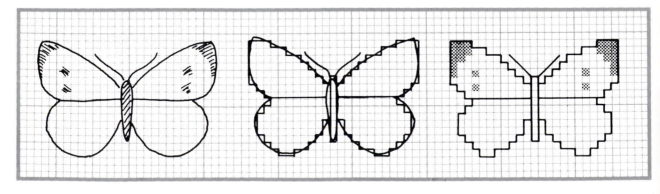

original line of the illustration, leaving the new, squared-up pattern ready to be coloured in (Fig 6). It is important to stay exactly on the lines of the graph paper; pencil lines which stray randomly into the spaces may make your drawing look better and more natural, but the pattern will be unsewable (Fig 7).

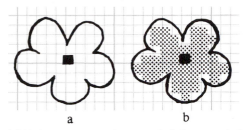

Fig 7 (a) This chart cannot be sewn in full cross stitch
(b) Only the shaded areas can be sewn in full cross stitch

You will notice that curved lines have been translated into a series of 'steps', because the pattern is now made up of squares. This angularity presents great difficulties in the designing of small things with subtle curving lines. Anything can be charted for cross stitch providing you are prepared to work on a large scale; the more squares you have to play with, ie the larger the finished design the more natural and realistic the result can be. So, if, after squaring-up, the design of your pet mouse looks more like a dented matchbox with whiskers (Fig 8a), there are two ways to get a better result. You can either make your design larger and allow more squares to achieve a better shape for your mouse (but its proportions by now will be elephantine, Fig 8b) or, if 'small is beautiful', design it using three-quarter cross stitch in addition to full cross stitch.

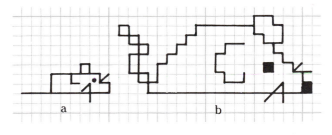

Fig 8 Mice, designed to be sewn using full cross stitches

THREE-QUARTER CROSS STITCH

The use of three-quarter cross stitch enables you to achieve more realism in a small design. If a full cross stitch forms a square shape when it is sewn, then a three-quarter cross stitch forms the shape of a right-angled triangle (Fig 9). If squares and right-angled triangles are combined in a design it is easier to suggest subtle shapes, and the eye can be fooled into thinking it sees curves and circles. A more recognisable mouse can now be charted on a smaller scale more befitting its size (Fig 10). Accuracy is still very important; with three-quarter cross stitch the pencil line must bisect the square exactly from corner to corner; there is no such thing as one-third cross stitch or other fractions, so make sure your pencil

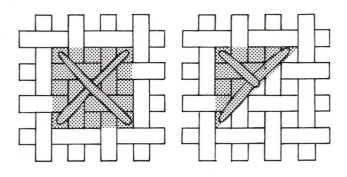

Fig 9 A full cross stitch forms a square shape when sewn; a three-quarter cross stitch forms a right-angled triangle

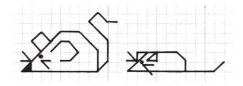

Fig 10 Mice, designed to be sewn using three-quarter cross stitch in addition to full cross stitch

line on the chart stays on the graph lines, or where you want to indicate the use of a three-quarter cross stitch, it must go diagonally across the square to form a right-angled triangle.

Even with the added possibilities afforded by the use of three-quarter cross stitch, complete accuracy and realism are not possible, nor are they desirable in this medium. Your design will be an interpretation of the event or subject you are portraying and if faithful accuracy is essential, hang a photograph on the wall instead. Allow yourself some artistic licence; include as much detail as you can to make your subject recognisable without cluttering your design unnecessarily. Do not worry if things are not exactly to scale; a study of old samplers shows little regard for scale and this only adds to their charm.

DETAILS

The use of back stitch and French knots allows the addition of small details to your cross stitch and can turn a meaningless small design into an instantly recognisable one (Fig 11).

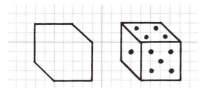

Fig 11 The addition of details, to be sewn in back stitch and French knots

Back stitch

Back stitch is most often used to outline something which would otherwise be indistinguishable from the background or from other areas of stitching. For example, a white house, stitched onto white linen, would be hard to see without outlining the side walls in a darker colour. Back stitch is also used where something needs to be emphasised, or for small details like mouths etc. It is invaluable for lettering where there is not enough space to allow the use of a cross-stitch alphabet.

The use of back stitch is indicated on a chart by means of a solid line. Every chart in this book has been outlined because you may choose to work the design in pale colours which require back stitching, but if the contrasts between colours are sufficient when you have sewn your designs you may not need to back stitch, so you can be selective and only outline where you feel it is necessary. Back stitch can break the rules about straying off the lines of the graph paper and can make use of any holes in the fabric covered by the design (see Chapter 4).

French knots

French knots are invaluable for eyes, buttons, badges, beads, musical notes and numerous other small details. They can appear singly, as in the case of eyes, or they can be grouped together in clusters to form bouquets of flowers, raspberries etc. Indicate their use on your chart by means of a small dot.

OFF-SETTING

Off-setting is a useful technique where a line rises neither vertically nor at an obliging angle of 45°, for example church steeples. As the line rises, rows of cross stitches can be placed half a square across on the chart, rather than a full square. At the sewing stage the off-set stitches are sewn one thread to the left or right of the previous stitching. Where more than one full cross stitch is involved, take care to off-set the whole row, not leaving a half stitch at the end of the row which will be unsewable. Fig 12 shows the top row of cross stitches off-set by one thread on the fabric (half a square on the chart). Study the fireman's helmet (Plate 42); the single cross stitch at the top is off-set in this manner.

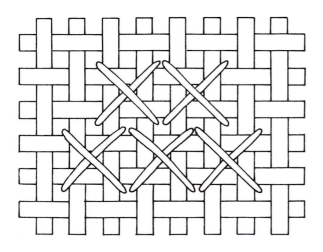

Fig 12 Off-setting a row of cross stitches

LETTERING

Draw out alphabets or words onto long strips of graph paper which will be cut to size later to fit the design. Do not worry too much about the spacing between letters and words; where you make a mistake simply cut the strip at the appropriate point and overlap to make the space smaller, or insert more paper to expand the word. This is generally quicker than erasing and re-drawing the lettering. There are no hard and fast rules about how many spaces to leave between letters and lines as alphabets vary so much in style and size. Draw out your lettering, look at it from a distance and trust your eye to tell you where you have gone wrong; it is then a simple matter to cut and make adjustments. To centre a strip of lettering onto your design, fold the strip to find the centre and line up this point with the central line of your design, thus avoiding a lot of counting. Lettering can be worked either in cross stitch or, where space is limited, in back stitch.

DESIGNING TO FIT AN EXISTING FRAME

If you are designing an embroidery to fit an existing frame you will have to do some mathematics to determine the maximum size of the piece of graph paper onto which you will fit all your design material (your master sheet).

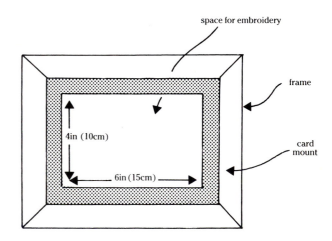

Fig 13 Measuring a frame to calculate the size of the master sheet

First measure the space inside the frame. Allow for a mount if you plan to use one and decide on the size of the space you wish to fill with the design. (If you are working in centimetres, 2.5cm equals 1in.) Next, count how many threads there are to 1in of the fabric you have chosen to sew on. Cross stitches are generally worked over two threads, so divide this number by 2 and you will get the number of cross stitches that will be worked on 1in of the fabric. Multiply the number of available inches by the number of crosses per inch to get the size of your master sheet. For example, if the space to be filled with embroidery measures 6in × 4in and the thread count gives you 10 cross stitches to 1in, multiply 6 × 10 = 60 and 4 × 10 = 40. Your master sheet, and consequently your finished design, must measure no more than 60 × 40 squares if the embroidery is to fit the frame (Fig 13).

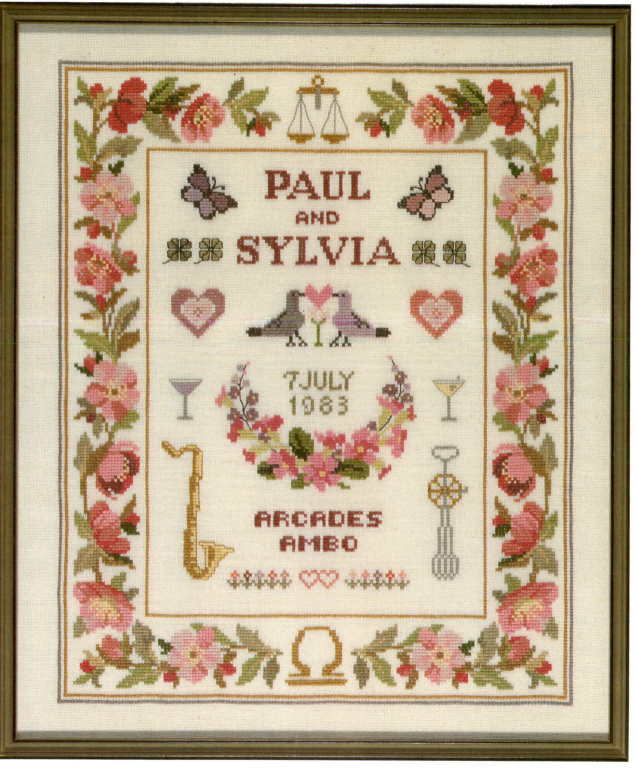

Plate 3 Courtship picture (sources, page 127)

If, however, you plan to have a frame made for the embroidery when it is completed, your master sheet can be of any size you choose.

BORDERS

A border is often necessary to provide a 'frame' for all the separate elements you have included in your design. The simplest border of all can be a single retaining line. Small designs generally look better with a narrow border, but with larger pieces of work you can be more ambitious. Draw out your border onto four long strips of graph paper to the approximate size you think you will need. To enlarge a border later, to fit around your design, add extra pattern repeats, and to make it smaller, cut the strips and remove the necessary number of repeats. Check that you have copied carefully and that the corners turn correctly; it is very discouraging to sew all the way round a border only to find that it does not join up. If you choose a band (Plate 66) as a basis for a continuous border, you will need to invent a corner. The simplest way to do this is with the help of a small hand mirror. Place the mirror on your band at an angle of 45° and move it along the band until a pleasing corner is reflected in the mirror. It is then a simple matter to draw out the new corner (Fig 14).

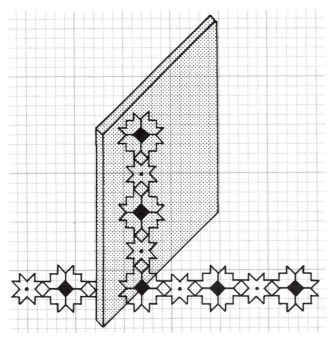

Fig 14 Using a hand mirror to invent a corner

Borders can also be formed using one, or more bands with or without a symbol in each corner (Fig 15). Where a pattern repeat slopes markedly in one direction it may be desirable to break the run at the centre of each side and reverse the pattern at this point to ensure four similar corners (Figs 16 and 17).

When you have drawn out your border, ask yourself if it would benefit from the addition of an inner and outer retaining line. A variety of borders and corners is shown in Plates 4 and 5.

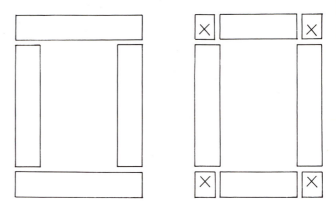

Fig 15 Placement of bands, or bands plus symbols (X) to form borders

CUTTING OUT THE DRAWINGS

As each separate ingredient of the design is completed, it is cut out ready to be positioned on the master sheet. Do not attempt to cut along the drawing line, this is far too fiddly and tedious. Aim to cut your drawings to rectangular or square-shaped pieces of paper, leaving a minimum of one clear square all around the drawing (Fig 18). As you cut out your drawings put them into an envelope for safe keeping until you have assembled all the items on your list.

ARRANGING THE DRAWINGS ON TO THE MASTER SHEET

Place all your drawings on the master sheet and shuffle them around to get a pleasing arrangement. Try several different layouts, change your mind as often as you like, for with this method you are free to do so without having to erase and re-draw each change. Position your border strips around the design and adjust the strips to fit if need be.

Be prepared to be flexible. If a particular item will not fit, or is out of character with the rest, it may be better to discard it for use on another occasion rather than to try and squeeze it in willy-nilly and risk spoiling your design. When you are finally satisfied with the placement of your drawings, fix them to the master sheet with adhesive, taking care to align the squares on the drawings with the squares on the master sheet. Consult Chapter 8 for more advice; it includes examples of how NOT to arrange design material which illustrate many mistakes.

COLOURING IN THE DESIGN

Colour in your design using coloured crayons. This will give you a fair idea of how the finished work will look before you have sewn a single stitch, giving the opportunity to make alterations, and will be a clear guide to colour changes when you are sewing.

Put your design on the wall, somewhere where you will see it frequently, and live with it for a week before you start to sew. If changes are needed they will soon become apparent, and they are easier to make at this stage. When you have lived happily with your design for a week you can start to sew it with confidence.

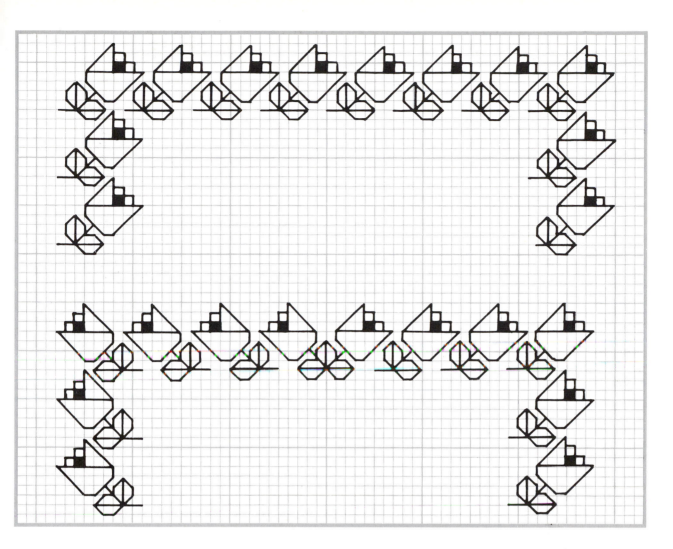

Fig 16 Reversing a pattern that slopes markedly in one direction

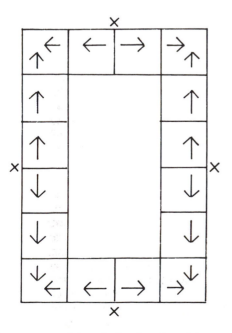

Fig 17 Pattern repeats slope in the direction of the arrows, and reversal points at X give the border four similar corners

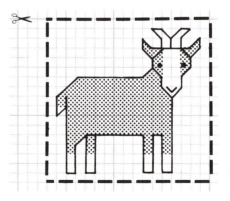

Fig 18 Cut out your drawings, allowing one clear square all round

17

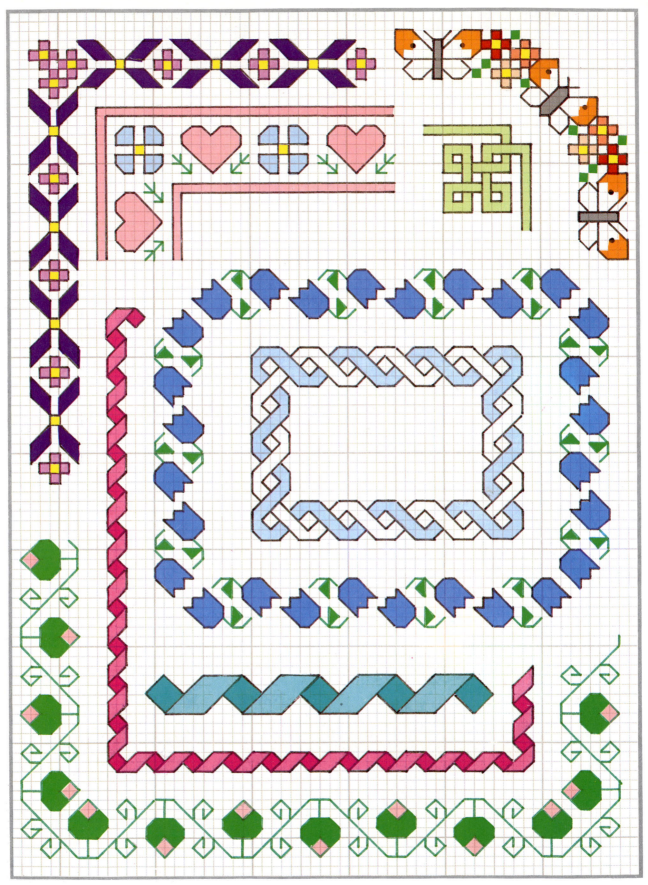

Plate 4

18

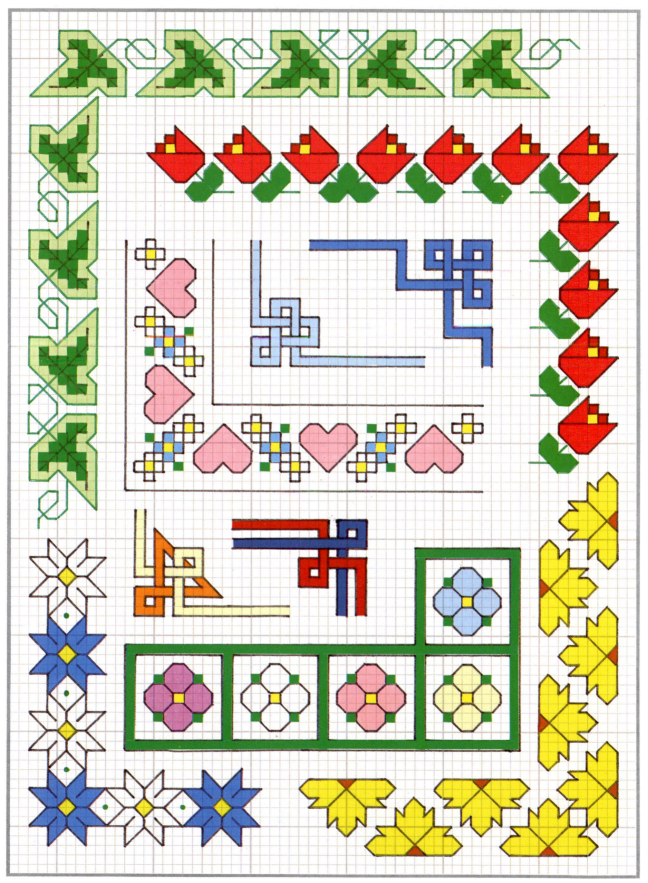

Plate 5

3 Preparing to Sew

Whilst your charted 'masterpiece' is pinned on the wall to see if it still meets with your approval after a week, use the time to acquire the materials you will need to sew it.

FABRIC

You will need a piece of fabric large enough to accommodate your sewn design, with enough spare fabric all round the edges to allow 2 to 3in (5 to 8cm) for turnings to be made when the finished embroidery is mounted and framed.

Fabrics for this work must have an even weave. This means that there must be the same number of weft (horizontal) threads as there are warp (vertical) threads to 1in (2.5cm). If the fabric is not evenweave, the designs you have drawn onto graph paper will be distorted in the sewing. Suitable evenweave fabrics can be either linen or cotton. The latter is cheaper, but whether you opt for linen or cotton, choose a count (see below) that will not strain your eyesight.

Evenweave linen

This fabric is woven with single threads (single weave) and has excellent qualities of durability and handling which are reflected in its high price. It is available in a variety of thread counts, a thread count being the number of threads there are to 1in (2.5cm). The smaller the number of such threads, the larger the weave is and the larger the cross stitch worked on it will be. Conversely, the higher the number of threads to 1in (2.5cm), the finer the fabric, and the smaller the cross stitches will be. As evenweave linen is made from natural linen fibres, some of the threads are coarser than others and the cross stitch is worked over two threads to even out any discrepancies. Thus, an evenweave linen with a thread count of 30 threads to 1in (2.5cm) will produce 15 cross stitches to 1in (2.5cm).

Hardanger

This is a cotton fabric available in many colours. It is not a single-weave fabric, but is woven instead with pairs of threads which give a denser background than a linen of the same thread count. The holes between the pairs of threads are easy to see and the count is usually 22 pairs of threads to 1in (2.5cm). When a cross stitch is worked over two pairs of threads, this fabric will produce 11 cross stitches to 1in (2.5cm).

Aida

This cotton fabric is woven to form a block of threads between each hole and the cross stitch is worked over one block. It comes in several counts; 18, 14, and 11 blocks to 1in (2.5cm) are readily available. This fabric is not suitable for a design which includes a lot of three-quarter cross stitches as there is no hole to accommodate the quarter stitch which is made over the half cross stitch. Where only a few three-quarter cross stitches appear in a pattern, it is possible to pierce a hole for the quarter stitch in the centre of the block of threads, using a sharp needle; but this is not a practice to be generally recommended.

HOW MUCH FABRIC TO BUY

If your eyes glaze over at the mention of mathematics and you are tempted to skip this section, be warned; mistakes in fabric shops can be very expensive.

When you have decided which fabric you are going to work on, make a note of its thread count and how many cross stitches will be produced to 1in (2.5cm). When making calculations always round figures up to the nearest ½in (1cm) as it is better to err on the side of generosity. Do not forget to add on a turning allowance of 3in (8cm) all round. Count the number of squares horizontally and vertically on your design. For the purposes of demonstration let us suppose that you have a design of 180 squares by 150 and that you have chosen to work on evenweave linen with a thread count of 30 threads to 1in. (If you are calculating in centimetres adjust these figures so that 1in represents 2.5cm.)

30 threads = 15 cross stitches to 1in

Divide the number of squares in your design by the number of cross stitches to 1in. For our example:

$$180 \div 15 = 12 \qquad 150 \div 15 = 10$$

Your finished embroidery will measure 12in × 10in. Add the turning allowance. You will need to buy a piece of fabric 18in × 16in (Fig 19).

If, however, you already have a piece of fabric and would like to design an embroidery to fit it, the calculations are the same as those that accompany Fig 13.

Before buying your fabric, check it for flaws. Sometimes a flaw can be covered by embroidery or can be lost in a turning, but do inspect the fabric carefully before it is cut from the roll. Check for dirty marks, particularly along creases, as it is better not to have to wash the fabric before you embroider it. Most fabric is expensive and comes in wide widths so you can either sew several designs onto one width, share with a friend, or look out for small off-cuts. When you buy your fabric ensure that the shop assistant cuts the fabric carefully along a thread line. If not, you will have to pull a thread out and cut again to straighten

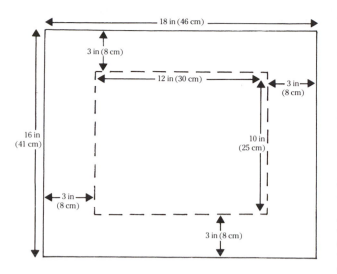

Fig 19 Calculating how much fabric to buy

it, which is irritating and wasteful.

When cutting a large piece of fabric into smaller ones always cut along a thread line and aim, if possible, to have the selvedge edge at the side edges of the embroidery. When the fabric has been cut to the desired size you will need to oversew the raw edges to prevent unravelling. This can be done by hand or using the zigzag stitch on a sewing machine. A hem is recommended if the work is to be mounted onto an embroidery frame whilst it is being worked, or onto hardboard for display; in both cases a hem will give a strong edge to support the lacing.

Find the centre of your fabric by folding it in half and then in half again. Mark the centre temporarily with a pin. Using a tacking thread in a contrasting colour, mark the centre lines on the fabric, from side to side and from top to bottom, through the centre mark, thus quartering your fabric (Fig 20). When you start to embroider, the central square of your design will need to be embroidered onto the centre mark, ensuring that your design fits onto the fabric exactly as planned.

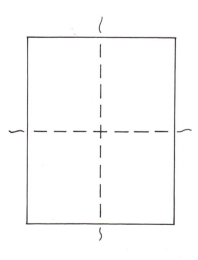

Fig 20 Quartering the fabric with tacking thread

THREADS

All the designs in this book were sewn using stranded cotton. Both D.M.C. and Anchor Mouline Stranded Cottons are readily available. These are six-stranded mercerised cottons with a lustrous finish which can be separated into single strands or groups of two or more strands. They are colour fast and are sold in 8m skeins. Dye-lots vary, so buy enough of each colour to finish your design. Gold and silver thread are useful when embroidering details such as buttons, jewellery, buckles etc. D.M.C. Fil d'Or (gold), or Fil d' Argent (silver), are suitable, as is the Danish Handcraft Guild gold and silver stranded thread.

Number of strands to use for different thread counts

Stitches must cover the ground sufficiently, but not be so thick that they enlarge the holes in the fabric. Remember that four cross stitches and a number of back stitches may all occupy the same hole. For 10 to 11 cross stitches to 1in (2.5cm), use 3 strands of stranded cotton for cross stitch, 2 strands for back stitch. For 12 to 17 cross stitches to 1in (2.5cm), use 2 strands of stranded cotton for cross stitch and 1 strand for back stitch. Work a few sample stitches in the corner of your fabric to check coverage.

Buying threads

Choice of colour is a very personal affair and there are no hard and fast rules. It might help to consider the room where the embroidery is to hang and build a colour scheme to harmonise with existing decoration and furnishings. Several shades of the same colour can sometimes be more effective than a completely random selection. If you doubt your own judgement look for a design whose colours you like in a book which gives a colour key. Make a note of the colour numbers for future reference; you will then know that these colours are pleasing to you and work well together. (Space has prevented the inclusion of colour keys in this book; the list for 'My Garden' (Plate 25), alone, would run to several pages. Although the emphasis is on personal designs and hence personal colour choices, you can of course use the colour photographs in this book as a guide when buying your threads.)

When you buy your threads find a well stocked shop with a large range of colours. Choose colours in full daylight. Hold them together in your hand to see if they harmonise with each other. Colours held in the hand can look brighter in the skein than when they are worked in small quantities alongside other colours. Lay the skeins on your fabric which will be the background and will in turn have an effect on the colours when they are embroidered onto it. Many people choose to imitate the pastel shades of old samplers, not realising that these colours are the result of years of fading. Originally they would have been quite bright; if you look closely at old samplers you will see that the pastel colours used originally have faded into complete obscurity, so if you are sewing for posterity avoid the very pale shades. If you are sewing on an off-white or cream-coloured fabric, very pale colours are hard to distinguish from the background. For this

Plate 6

reason you may have to choose deeper shades than your original choice, but the colours can still be soft as there are many deeper shades that are neither harsh nor garish.

To avoid losing spare strands after you have cut a length from the skein and have separated the strands, make yourself a thread holder. Old greetings cards with holes punched down the sides can be threaded with spare thread, and it is a good idea to write the shade number beside each occupied hole for future reference (Fig 21).

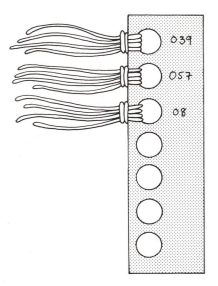

Fig 21 A thread holder

OTHER ITEMS

Needles
You will need a blunt tapestry needle which will slip easily through the holes in your fabric without piercing or splitting the threads. The needle should be sufficiently fine to slip through the holes without enlarging or distorting them. Finer needles have a higher number on the packet (26), thicker needles have lower numbers (18). Buy several; they get lost and have been known to break.

Scissors
You will need dressmaking scissors if you are going to cut your fabric to size before sewing, and a pair of sharp, fine-pointed embroidery scissors. The latter will be used for cutting thread from the skein and when finishing off a thread in the embroidery. If they are not sharp they will 'chew' the thread. Messy finishing on the back of the work is to be avoided as it can show through on the right side when the work is mounted. Embroidery scissors are also used for, horror of horrors, unpicking. The points must be fine enough to slip under the offending stitch to cut it. Never be tempted to use a stitch ripper as this will distort your existing stitching and your fabric. When sewing, hang your embroidery scissors around your neck on a ribbon, which saves hunting for them every time they are put down.

Hoops
The use of a hoop ensures that you produce accurate and even stitching and that the minimum amount of pressing will be necessary when the work is completed. Use a hoop only if the whole area to be stitched fits easily inside it. If the hoop has to be moved over existing embroidery the stitches risk being flattened and distorted by the pressure of the hoop, so for larger embroideries use a frame.

Circular hoops come in many sizes and consist of two wooden, plastic or metal rings (Fig 22). The fabric is placed over the inner ring, the outer ring is placed on top and is tightened with a screw adjuster so that the fabric is stretched taut (Fig 23). Ensure that the weave of the fabric is square with the screw adjuster and that the screw is at

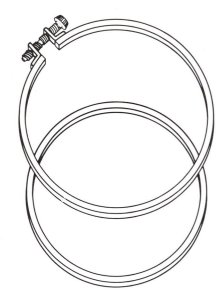

Fig 22 A hoop

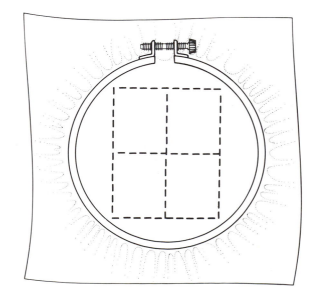

Fig 23 Fabric mounted onto a hoop

the top of your work to keep it out of your way and to stop threads catching on it as you sew. The work is done with a stabbing motion, the needle being inserted from front to back, pulled through and then inserted from back to front and pulled through again. To protect the fabric and prevent it slipping, the inner hoop should be bound with a white bias tape, held in place at the end with a few stitches (Fig 24).

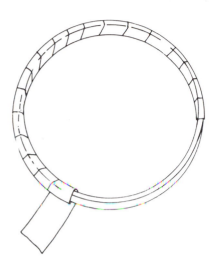

Fig 24 Binding the inner hoop

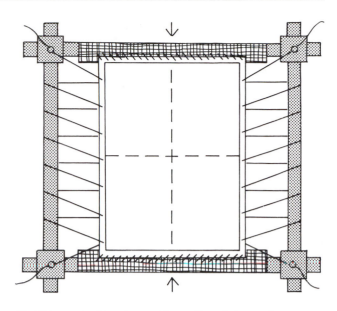

Fig 25 An embroidery frame, 'dressed' ready for work

Frames

Frames serve the same purpose as hoops and are used for larger pieces of work which will not fit inside a hoop. Rectangular frames come in many sizes, some of the larger ones have a floor-stand allowing you to hold one hand at the front of the work and one at the back, which speeds up the stabbing motion. They consist of two wooden stretchers at the side and two wooden rollers held in place by wing-nuts or pegs. The rollers each have a piece of webbing nailed to them. The fabric must be no wider than the webbing, if it is you will need a larger frame. The fabric can be of any length as the excess is wound onto the rollers when it is not being worked.

To set up the frame for work, first hem your fabric to give it strong edges that will not pull apart when it is laced to the frame. Sew the top of the fabric to the top piece of webbing and do the same at the bottom, matching the centre of the fabric to the centre of the webbing. Put the frame together and tighten the pegs or wing-nuts. Lace the sides of the fabric to the stretchers with a strong thread or fine cord and, when both sides are laced, tighten the laces so that the fabric is stretched taut. Tie the ends of the laces firmly to the stretchers. Your frame is now 'dressed', ready for work (Fig 25).

Cross-stitch embroidery can be worked without the aid of hoops and frames. The work is held in the hand and the stitching is done with a continuous stitching motion which some find quicker than the stabbing movement required by the use of a hoop or frame. When embroidering without a hoop or frame it is essential that you work with a good, even tension, taking great care not to pull the thread so tight that the holes in the fabric are enlarged and distorted, nor to work so slackly that the stitches flap about on the surface of the fabric.

Lighting

Trying to embroider in the gloom results in tired eyes, followed often by the discouragement of having to unpick mistakes. Sit near a window to work during daylight hours. Those who are tempted to sew outdoors on a fine day are in peril of staining their work; beware of perspiring fingers, children lurching around with ice creams and the less obvious danger of a bird with an upset stomach flying overhead. When sewing at night, work under a good lamp, positioned on your left if you are right-handed, and on your right if you are left-handed, so that you are not working in your own shadow. Use a magnifier if necessary. This can be on a stand or can hang around your neck; some models even have a built-in light. If you are still struggling to see the work clearly, give in gracefully and go and have your eyes tested.

4 Sewing the Design

The main stitch used in the sewing of your design will be full cross stitch. You will also need to know how to form a three-quarter cross stitch, how to back stitch and how to make French knots. Practise any stitches which are unfamiliar to you before you begin to sew your design.

STITCHES

Full cross stitch

One completely filled square on your chart indicates one full cross stitch on your fabric. When working on even-weave linen or cotton, work the full cross stitch over two threads (Fig 26), on Hardanger over two pairs of threads (Fig 27), and on Aida over one block of threads (Fig 28).

When working rows of full cross stitches, bring the needle out at the left-hand side of the row of stitches to be worked. Insert the needle two threads up and two threads across. Pull the thread through to the back. Bring the needle out two threads down. A half cross has been formed and you are ready to work the next stitch in the

Fig 28 A full cross stitch worked on Aida

line. Continue working half crosses until the end of the line is reached, then return making the complete crosses, working from right to left and using the same holes as before (Fig 29). All stitches interlock or 'hold hands', sharing holes with their neighbours, unless they are single stitches worked on their own.

Fig 26 A full cross stitch worked on evenweave linen

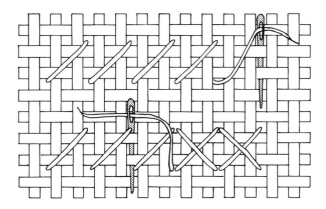

Fig 29 Working a line of full cross stitches

Fig 27 A full cross stitch worked on Hardanger

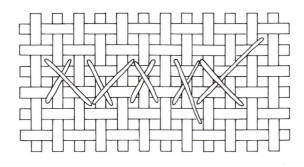

*Fig 30 How **not** to do it*

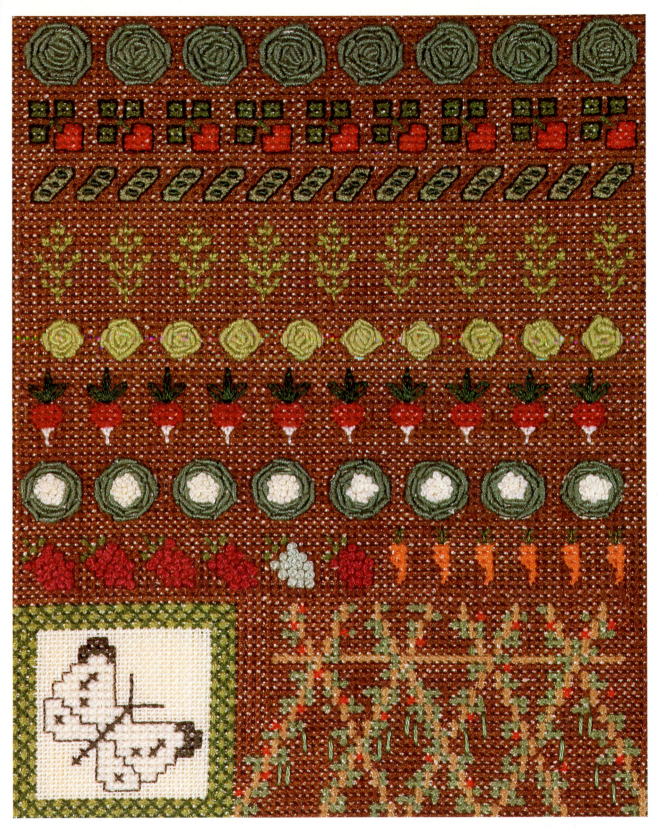

Plate 7 Detail from 'My Garden' (see page 67), showing the use of full cross stitch, three-quarter cross stitch, back stitch, French knots and bullion bars

Fig 33 Two three-quarter cross stitches, sewn back to back

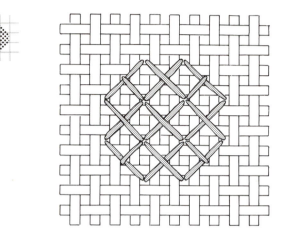

Fig 31 Spaces on the chart indicate bare fabric

The first few stitches are sometimes confusing but you will soon become accustomed to seeing threads in pairs and mistakes will become obvious (Fig 30). Spaces on the chart indicate unworked ground, ie bare fabric, so for each space leave two threads uncovered (Fig 31).

It is important that the bottom stitch slants in the same direction throughout the work; if your bottom stitches all slant from left to right, your top stitches will automatically all slant from right to left, giving your work a regular appearance and a pleasing sheen. It does not matter which direction you choose – whichever comes most naturally is best – so long as you are consistent. Take care if you turn your work sideways, when embroidering a border for instance; a large full cross stitch worked as a sample in the turning allowance will show you at a glance which way your bottom stitch should be lying.

Three-quarter cross stitch

This will be indicated on your chart by a right-angled

Fig 32 Four examples of three-quarter cross stitch

Fig 34 A combination of full cross stitch and three-quarter cross stitch

triangle. The first half of the cross stitch is formed in the usual way but the second 'quarter' stitch is brought across and down into the central hole (Fig 32). The rule of having the bottom stitches always slanting in the same direction is thus sometimes broken, but by bringing the 'quarter' stitch over the top, the longer bottom stitch is anchored down firmly giving a neater effect. Where the chart indicates two three-quarter stitches together, these are worked sharing the same central hole and occupying the space of one whole cross stitch (Fig 33). Fig 34 shows a combination of full cross stitch and three-quarter cross stitch.

Back stitch

The use of back stitch is indicated on your chart by a solid line. When all the full and three-quarter cross stitches have been worked in one area of the design, back stitch can be worked around or over them to add detail and definition. It can also be used to work lettering. Back stitch is worked either over two threads or one, depending on the direction indicated on the chart. It can be worked vertically, horizontally or diagonally. Bring the needle out at 1 and in again at 2. Bring it out again at 3 and in again at 4 (Fig 35). Continue this sequence in the direction indicated by your chart (Fig 36).

A white tennis ball, when sewn onto a light-coloured fabric, requires both outlining for definition and detailing

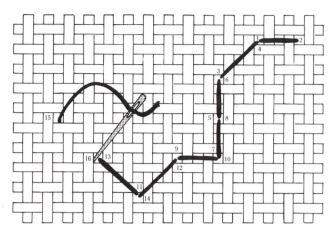

Fig 35 Back stitch

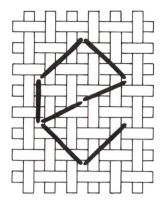

Fig 38 Back stitch can be worked both over two threads or, occasionally, over one

Fig 36 Back stitch used for lettering

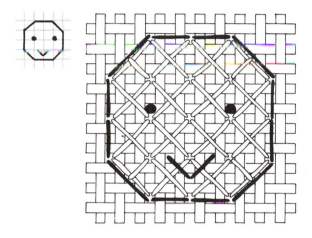

Fig 39 Stitching a face

Fig 37 Back stitch used for definition and detail

to distinguish it from a golf ball (Fig 37). For added versatility back stitch can be worked over two threads in one direction and one thread in another (Fig 38). Sometimes the unused holes within the cross stitches are used, for example when sewing mouths onto faces, the stitch in

this case being sewn over one thread (Fig 39).

A single back stitch can be used on its own for details such as whiskers on cats etc. Always use fewer strands of thread for back stitch than you have used for the cross stitches.

French knots

The use of this stitch will be indicated on your chart by a dot. To sew a French knot, bring the needle out one thread to the right of where you want the knot to lie. Depending on the size of the knot you require, slip the needle once or twice under the thread so that the twists lie snugly around the needle. Without allowing the thread to untwist, insert the needle back into the fabric one thread to the left of where you started and pull the thread through to the back (Fig 40). If you do not work the knot with one thread to support it, you risk the knot sinking into the hole and getting lost on the back of the work.

Work French knots with one strand of thread. For larger knots try using two strands or try a thicker needle. Too many twists around the needle will not produce a satisfactory round knot, so experiment beforehand to get the effect you want.

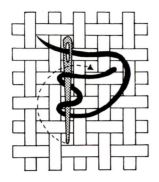

Fig 40 Working a French knot

Bullion bars

Bullion bars have been used to work the cabbages, lettuces and cauliflowers in the garden picture (Plates 7 and 25) where they add texture and relief to a large expanse of cross stitch. To sew a bullion bar, bring the needle out at A and, leaving a long loop of thread, re-insert the needle at B, which will determine the length of the bar. Bring the needle out again at A. Wrap the loop of thread six or more times around the needle depending on the length of the bar. Pull the needle through the twists, holding them carefully and stroking them down in the direction A to B. To finish, re-insert your needle at B again (Fig 41). Practise making bullion bars on spare fabric if you have never tried them before.

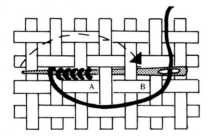

Fig 41 Working a bullion bar

HOW TO START AND FINISH WITHOUT A KNOT

Where a new colour butts up against existing stitches, the new thread can be run through the back of two or three of the stitches already worked. Make a small back stitch to secure it and bring the new thread to the right side to start work.

When starting a new thread in bare fabric, where there are no existing stitches onto which the new thread can be anchored, another technique is needed. Insert the needle at A, leaving a short tail on the front of the work. Bring the needle out at B where the stitching is to start. Stitch in the direction of A, catching the thread at the back as you sew (Fig 42). After a few stitches the thread will be secure and the loose end can be trimmed off neatly on the back of the work (Fig 43).

To finish without using a knot, run the thread through the backs of three or four stitches which have just been worked, taking care not to distort them. Take a small back stitch to secure the end and cut off the thread close to the fabric (Fig 44).

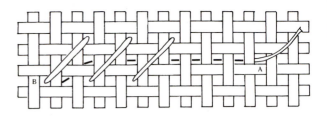

Fig 42 Starting without the use of a knot (right side of fabric)

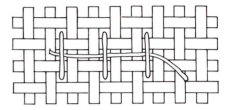

Fig 43 Starting without the use of a knot (wrong side of fabric)

Fig 44 Finishing without the use of a knot (wrong side of fabric)

STARTING TO SEW YOUR DESIGN

Your first stitch will be the central stitch on your chart and will be sewn in the centre of your fabric, which you have already marked with tacking threads. If the central square on your chart happens to be a blank space, you will have to count from the centre to the nearest area to be stitched and begin there. To count accurately across areas of bare fabric it is easiest to thread your needle with tacking thread and, counting carefully, work the correct number of dummy crosses to the point where you wish to start. With the correct position found you can later remove the tacking-thread crosses, leaving only the intended spaces.

When the first piece of your design is correctly positioned on your fabric, you are free to proceed in any direction you choose. Some people like to work the border early on, others leave it to the end. When sewing the border, check your work frequently as you progress, for it can be very disheartening to find you have mis-counted and the border will not join up.

Test piece

To ensure that beginners will be able to translate the designs in this book into embroidery, a test piece is included which can be studied and worked (Plate 8). The figure chosen includes the use of full cross stitch and three-quarter cross stitch, with back stitch and French knots for details, thus covering the main techniques. So that your work can be put to good use, alter the colours to suit someone you know, and you will have the beginnings of a greetings card for her. When you are satisfied that

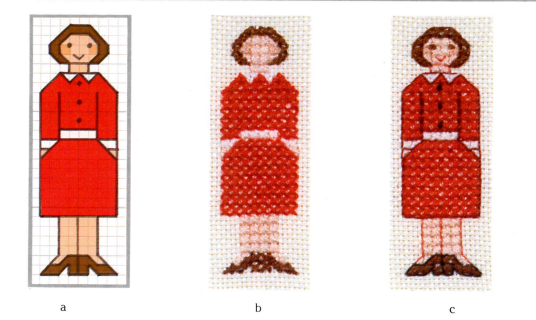

a   b   c

Plate 8 Test piece. Working from the chart (a), first sew all the full cross stitches and three-quarter cross stitches (b), then add back stitch and French knots to complete your figure (c)

your embroidered figure compares favourably with the example shown here, you will be able to tackle with confidence any design in this book.

DOS AND DON'TS
- Do wash your hands before each work session.
- Do press any stubborn creases out of your fabric before you embroider your first stitch. When the work is complete it will only need a light pressing to avoid flattening the stitches.
- Do finish off neatly after each separate area has been worked. Thread can be brought from one area to another across the back of the work, without finishing off, only if there is an existing line of stitching behind which the thread can be hidden. Take care not to distort existing stitches as you bring your thread through the backs of these stitches.
- Do cut off threads close to the fabric with sharp embroidery scissors.
- Do cut off loose ends immediately before they get caught up in other work.
- Do use sharp embroidery scissors and tweezers to remove mistakes.
- Do allow the needle to dangle upside down from the fabric occasionally to remove any twists on the thread. Threads cover better when lying flat, a twisted thread will give uneven stitches.
- Do roll your embroidery in acid free tissue when it is not being worked and protect it from accidents. If it is on a

hoop or frame, cover it well between work sessions to keep it clean.
- Do leave until last all areas to be stitched in white thread, to keep them clean and sparkling.
- Do relax and enjoy your work.

- Don't leave your needle in the fabric when you put it away. It could leave a mark or rust if left for any length of time.
- Don't use more than 12in (30cm) of thread in your needle. It will twist and tangle and the end near the needle will be worn before you use it.
- Don't work the background. In cross-stitch embroidery the ground is left bare.
- Don't jump your thread across the back of bare fabric from one area to another. When the work is mounted, a trail will be visible through the fabric and will spoil its appearance.
- Don't pull the fabric threads together by tugging too hard on the needle as you sew; lacy holes belong in pulled-thread work, not in cross-stitch embroidery.
- Don't sew with unpicked thread. It will be worn and kinked.
- Don't use a stitch ripper to remove mistakes. You will distort your fabric and existing stitches.
- Don't fold your work for storage. Stubborn creases will develop which will be difficult to remove and will eventually weaken the fabric.
- Don't use knots for starting and finishing. They can come undone and will form unsightly lumps when the work is mounted.
- Don't forget to remove any tacking threads.
- Don't be surprised if you become addicted to this work.

5 Decorated Initials

For a simple first project, which is not too daunting, start with a decorated initial. Choose that of a friend, decorate it with a relevant symbol, and you will have made an original and acceptable gift. Being small, initials are quick and satisfying to produce and will hopefully give you the confidence to continue with something more ambitious. The designs in this chapter offer two alphabets from which to choose your initial, and examples of how these initials can be used to produce a personalised result.

THE LARGE ALPHABET

The Large Alphabet (Fig 46) has been designed to be accompanied by a symbol of your choice, the only decoration on it being small flowers which are easily removed if you want to leave the letter plain. These letters can be used singly, as decorated initials, or can be put together into names or messages.

How to decorate an initial

Examples of how to decorate an initial are shown in Fig 45. First choose your initial and draw it out onto graph paper. Next choose the decorative symbol you want to use with the initial. You may wish to invent your own or you may prefer to look through this book to find something suitable. Draw out your symbol onto another small piece of graph paper and cut it out. Move the symbol from side to side over the initial until you find a good position for it. You will notice that most of the letters have at least one thick upright section and this is generally a good position. Where there is more than one upright you may like to use more than one symbol. Take care that whatever you choose, it does not obliterate the initial and make it unrecognisable.

If you wish to use one of the symbols in the examples, but it appears on an initial which is not the one you want, draw out your initial and add the symbol to the new initial trying to get it on a similar upright section of the letter. When you are happy with the positioning of your symbol, stick it into place over the initial. Tidy up the drawing and colour it in. Your pattern is now ready to sew.

Examples (Fig 45)

'D' For a gardener; position a trowel and a watering can on any initial. As flowers are appropriate to the theme, as many as possible can be left in place.

'E' For a cat lover, sit a cat in front of an upright section of any initial. The shape of some letters will give you room to add a kitten.

'V' For someone who likes flowers or maybe for someone called Violet, place a small violet on any initial and add a few leaves.

'M' For a needleworker, position an embroidery frame on an upright section of any initial. The flowers can be left in place for added decoration.

'A' Again for a needleworker, but a different approach this time. The embroidery frame (Plate 68) can be drawn out, and any initial from the Floral Alphabet (Plate 9) can be drawn onto the frame to look like a piece of embroidery.

'P' For a railway enthusiast or a child, position a train on any initial. The flowers can be removed to allow the addition of some steam. A signal can be added if there is space.

'I' For a child, place some toys with any initial. As the symbols do not obscure a lot of the initial, the flowers can be left in place.

'N' For a musician or violinist, place a violin over the upright section of any initial and scatter a few musical notes around.

'S' For a birthday treat, add a birthday cake with candles alight and a present. 'S' is an example of an initial with no single upright section, so the symbols have been placed either side of the centre section.

'W' For a cricketer, use the uprights of any initial as a background for the cricket bat, ball and stumps.

'F' For the very young, lean a baby against an initial and fill any gaps with bricks.

'T' For a keen knitter, position a piece of knitting on the upright and make it narrower than the original in the Pattern Library to fit the initial.

'U' For a child, baby, or perhaps for Ursula, as the name means 'little bear'. Position a teddy bear on an upright of your chosen initial.

THE FLORAL ALPHABET (Plate 9)

You may like to experiment adding different flowers and butterflies to the initial of your choice; the flowers are interchangeable, as are the butterflies.

The letters can also be used to spell out names, an example of the name 'Betty' is shown at the bottom of the chart. Many names have the same letter used more than once in them, and rather than sew the same pattern twice, and to give variety, change the repeated letter by taking a flower from another letter and substituting it for the one you have already used. As the name 'Betty' has five letters, and five flowers are given in the pattern, it was decided to include an example of each, which required some

Fig 45 How to place a symbol with an initial

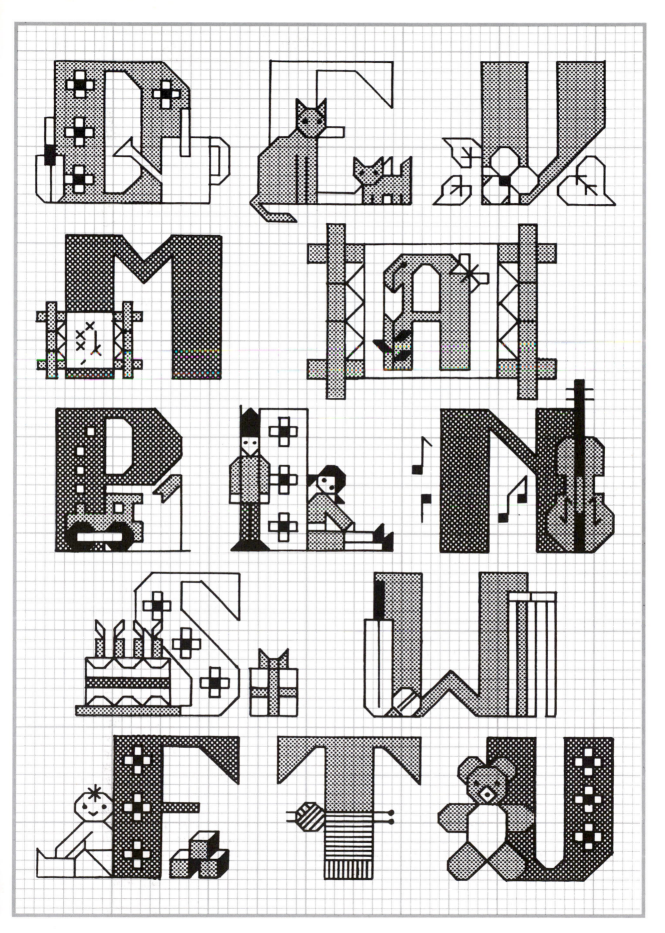

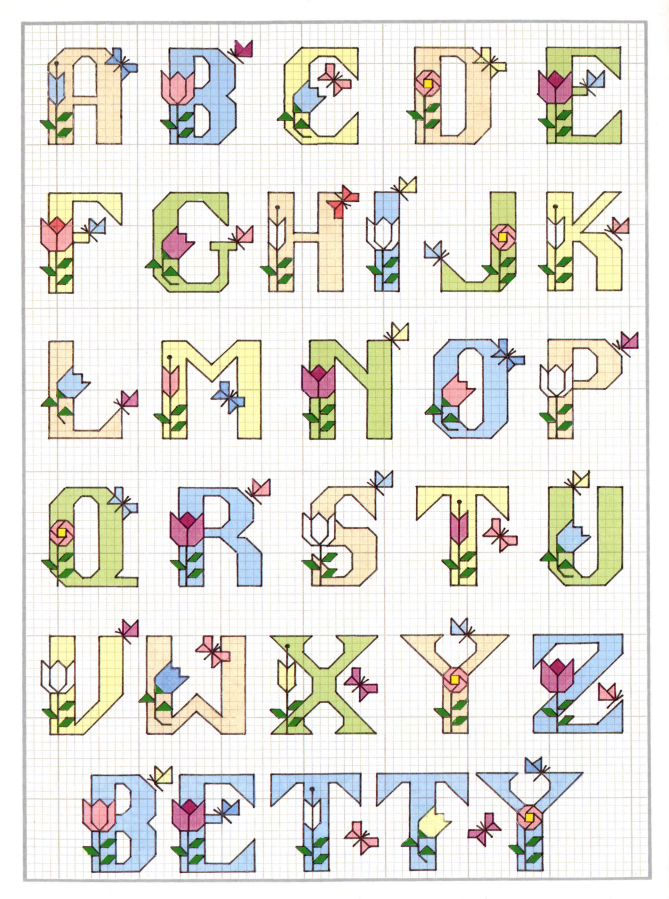

Plate 9 Floral alphabet

Plate 10 My daughter's name, decorated with wild flowers (sources, page 127)

rearrangement as you will see from the chart. Use the butterflies to fill any spaces created by the positioning of the letters, and check that all your butterflies are not flying in the same direction.

EMBROIDER A GUEST TOWEL

Evenweave fabric can now be bought as a ribbon, ie a long thin strip, sold by the metre and which usually has a decorative coloured edging. Onto this can be embroidered any wording or narrow design you choose. The ribbon which has been sewn onto the guest towel has been embroidered with the word 'Welcome' (Plate 12).

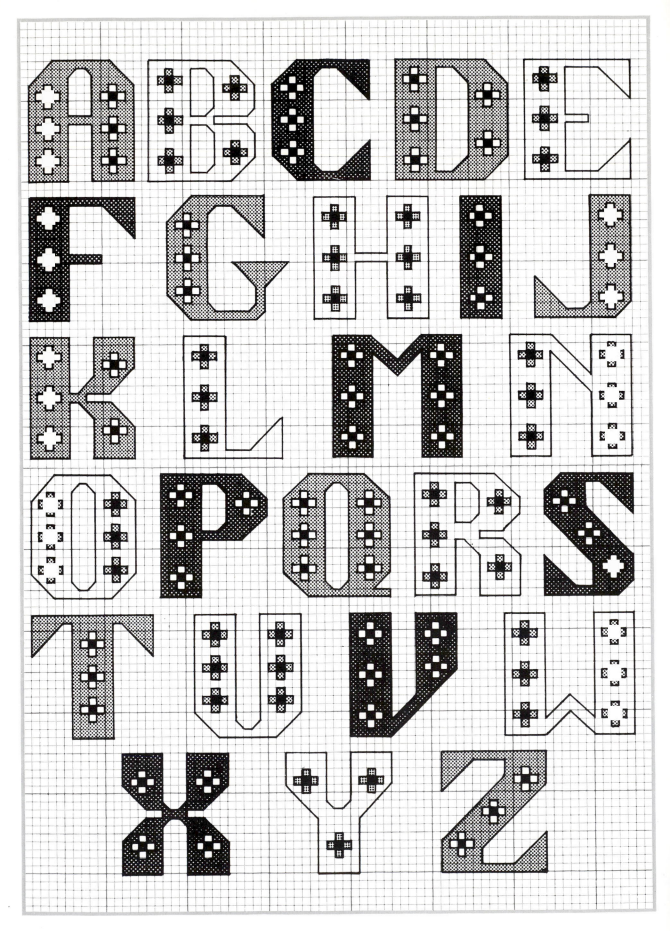

Letters from the Large Alphabet (Fig 46) were drawn out onto graph paper and the only addition was a small band of matching flowers positioned either side of the word. When the embroidery was complete, the ribbon was sewn to the towel. When you come to sew your own design, centre it onto the ribbon.

MAKE A NEEDLE CASE

The needle case (Plate 12) was designed for a friend who is an expert at patchwork and quilting. The samples of patchwork in the Pattern Library were put together and repeated to form a border, and her initial was adapted from the Large Alphabet (Fig 46) to fit the space and to accommodate the patchwork flower pot. Any border, initial and symbol of your choice can be substituted.

To make a needle case the same size as mine, you will need a piece of fabric 14in (35cm) by 3½in (9cm). Using the calculations in Chapter 2, adjust the size of your master sheet to suit the thread count of the fabric you have chosen, in order to ensure that your design will fit onto the front section of your needle case. In other words, work out how many cross stitches will fit the space available and make your design no larger than that.

The shaded area in Fig 47 shows the position for the embroidery on the fabric. When the embroidery is complete fold the fabric in half, A to A, right sides together, and seam from A to B and from C to D, leaving an opening between B and C (Fig 47). Re-fold the fabric as shown in

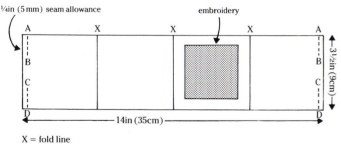

Fig 47 Layout of fabric for a needle case

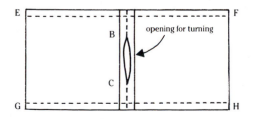

Fig 48 Seam lines on a needle case

Fig 48, still with the right sides together, and seam from E to F and from G to H. Turn the needle case the right way out and slip-stitch the opening, which will be on the central fold inside the needle case and hidden from view when the leaves are in place. Insert leaves of felt fabric to

Fig 46 The Large Alphabet

hold the needles and finish off with a plait of embroidery thread, tied in a bow, to hold the leaves in place.

STITCH A NAPKIN RING (Plate 12)

The fabric used is Hardanger and the results have stood up to years of laundering in this household. Each ring consists of a strip of fabric onto which the initial is embroidered, and is formed into a napkin ring using press fasteners. The best press fasteners for the job are the kind that you hammer in, though the ordinary sewn-on variety are adequate. You will need a piece of Hardanger 6in (15cm) by 4in (10cm), though you may substitute any evenweave fabric with a thread count which will produce 11 cross stitches to 1in (2.5cm).

Choose an initial from this chapter or from the Nursery Alphabet (Plate 35). Centre your chosen initial onto the fabric (Fig 49). When it is embroidered, fold the fabric A to A, right sides together and seam from A to C and from B to D (Fig 50). Re-fold the fabric, still with right sides together (Fig 51), and seam from E to F and from G to H.

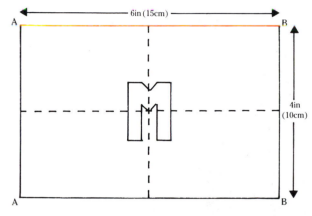

Fig 49 Layout of fabric for a napkin ring

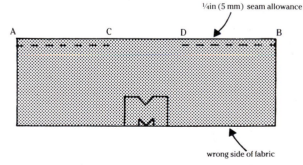

Fig 50 Seam from A to C and from B to D

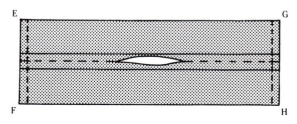

Fig 51 Seam from E to F and from G to H

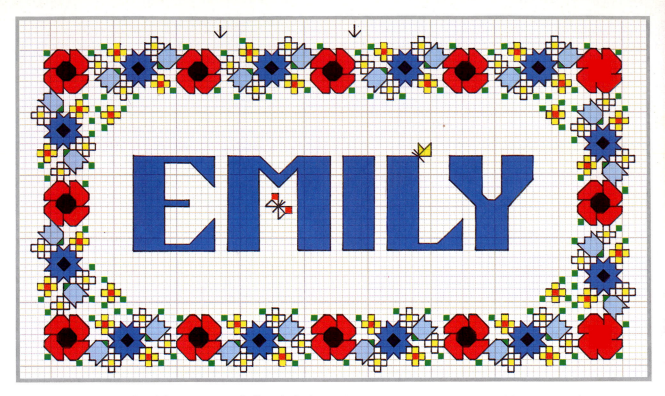

Turn the napkin ring the right way out and slip-stitch the opening. Attach press fasteners (Fig 52).

There is just one word of warning; if you make these for house guests to use whilst they are staying with you, they invariably ask to take them home as a reminder of their visit.

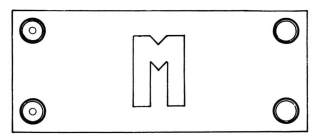

press fasteners

Fig 52 Attach press fasteners to the finished napkin ring

DECORATE A BOX LID

There are many boxes with lids designed to hold a small piece of embroidery, available from craft shops and needlework shops. The lid of the box in Plate 12 contains a 'V' for Verso taken from this chapter. If the box has a circular lid take care to ensure that your design will fit the space available when it is sewn; measure the diameter of the circle of fabric that will be visible and work out how many cross stitches will fit this space. Use the calculations in Chapter 2 to help you and adjust the size of your master sheet accordingly. When the embroidery is complete and has been pressed, follow the instructions for mounting, which should be supplied by the box manufacturer.

△ *Plate 11 Floral border, adjustable to surround any name*

SURROUND A NAME WITH FLOWERS

If you choose to embroider a name made up of letters from the Large Alphabet, you may like to enclose the name with a floral border. A border of cornflowers, poppies and other flowers is included in this chapter and can be altered to fit any length of name. The name chosen for the example was 'Emily' (Plate 11); the letters were taken from the Large Alphabet and were drawn out onto graph paper. The border was drawn out onto separate long strips of graph paper which were positioned around the name. This border consists of pattern repeats (one whole pattern repeat is marked on the chart), and a few extra flowers are added to soften the corners. If you are working on a short name you will need to make the border smaller. Simply use less pattern repeats at the top and the bottom. Conversely, for a longer name, add more pattern repeats to get a suitably sized border.

FRAME AN INITIAL

There are many small frames on the market which add the finishing touch to a small piece of embroidery. Take care that your design will fit your chosen frame. Again, use the calculations in Chapter 2 and adjust the size of your master sheet accordingly.

Any initial with any decoration, with or without a border, can be placed in a small frame. 'J', for Jill, has been taken from the Large Alphabet (Fig 46). As butterflies are my 'signature', and as this was a personal gift to a friend, butterflies have been used to make a border (Plate 12). To copy this border use the butterflies on Plate 4, repeating the pattern four times to form a circle.

Plate 12

Accept this ❀ trifle
❀❀ from a friend ❀❀
Whose love for you
❀ will never end.

6 Greetings Cards

For a special greetings card, that you know will be treasured and kept long after it is given, consider producing your own design, tailor-made for its recipient.

Patterns to suit many occasions are included in this chapter. Some can be sewn as they stand, others need only the alteration of some lettering or the addition of a date. Where the design consists of a circular floral border, any greeting you choose can be placed in the middle. Greetings and lettering for different relatives have been drawn out for you (Fig 55). Where a name or a word of your choice is too long to fit the space, re-draw the lettering using a smaller alphabet. Alternatively, consider leaving only one thread bare between letters, instead of the usual two, when you come to sew the word. More can be squeezed into a small space using this technique. The smallest alphabet in this book, alphabet 7 (Fig 55) makes use of only nine holes in the fabric. To sew a 'W', for example, bring your needle out at 1 and in at 3, out at 5 and in at 3, out at 5 and in at 9, out at 7 and in at 9 (Fig 53).

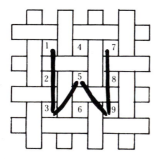

Fig 53 Stitching the letter 'W' from alphabet 7 (Fig 55)

HAPPY BIRTHDAY (Plates 13 and 15)
This design of a circle of flowers can be stitched in any colours you choose; you might take your cue from the season of the year in which the birthday falls: yellow, white and pale blue for spring; stronger colours for summer; shades of gold and orange for autumn; and red, white and green for winter. Alter the greeting if you wish; there is room here for a short name to make it more personal. If the name is too long to fit the space, try using a smaller alphabet for the lettering, or omit the name and move the words HAPPY BIRTHDAY down to fill the space. For a wedding anniversary draw out the words HAPPY 25TH ANNIVERSARY (or whatever number you need). The word ANNIVERSARY (Fig 55) will fit into the circle if one thread instead of two is left bare between the letters when you sew them. Or you can re-draw the message using a smaller alphabet. Use colours to suit the occasion: silver,

white and pale blues for a Silver Wedding; yellows and gold for a Golden Wedding, and rich reds for a Ruby Wedding.

HAPPY CHRISTMAS (Plates 14 and 15)
Space has been left on Santa's sack for you to add the initial of a family or a child; any of the smaller alphabets can be used. Add the words HAPPY CHRISTMAS if you like; they are drawn out for you ready to use (Fig 55). If you use silver or gold thread to sew a retaining line around the whole design, or to sew the buckle on the belt, you will add some festive sparkle.

The circle of flowers for the birthday card can be used for a Christmas card if the colours chosen are a seasonable red, white, green and gold.

WELL DONE (Plates 14 and 15)
A card to congratulate success in examinations. If you want to wish someone GOOD LUCK instead, change the message using the words drawn out for you (Fig 55). Alter the appearance of the candidate using different physical features to be found in the Pattern Library and add a name, or the date of the ordeal.

HAPPY MOTHER'S DAY (Plates 13 and 15)
A circle of spring flowers has been designed; this can be used for almost any occasion if the greeting is altered. Replace the wording with HAPPY EASTER if you wish, and again, add a name or a date perhaps.

VALENTINE (Plates 14 and 15)
Cupid is standing in a floral heart preparing to shoot an arrow. Use alphabet 6 (Fig 55) to make the initials placed either side of Cupid appropriate to your needs. Another romantic approach would be to stitch the words BE MINE inside one of the floral circles and incorporate a heart or two into the design.

GET WELL SOON (Plates 14 and 15)
The sufferer is in bed, but she is smiling and on the mend. Alter the hair style to suit the patient; many examples of hair styles can be found in the Pattern Library and can be used to replace this one. The potty under the bed is optional. Alternatively, the words GET WELL SOON can be inserted into any of the circular floral borders in this chapter. Add the patient's name to make the card even more of a tonic.

Fig 54 Alphabets 1 to 5

no 1

no 2

no 3

no 4

no 5

Plate 13

42

Plate 14

no 6

ABCDEFGHIJKLMN
OPQRSTUVWXYZ
1234567890   123456789

no 7   ABCDEFGHIJKLMNOPQRSTUVWXYZ

DEAR — SISTER — BROTHER
FATHER — DAD — DAUGHTER
MOTHER—MUM—SON—GRANNY
GRANDAD —COUSIN —FRIEND
UNCLE—AUNT—NEPHEW—NIECE
BEST WISHES — ! ? — IN-LAW
HAPPY CHRISTMAS/EASTER
NEW YEAR/ANNIVERSARY
TO........WITH LOVE FROM
THANK YOU — GOOD LUCK

WELCOME TO YOUR NEW HOME (Plates 13 and 15)
'Daisies pied and violets blue' – this is another circle of flowers suitable for any occasion if the message is changed.

WELCOME BABY (Plates 13 and 15)
This needs only the addition of the new baby's name. Providing you avoid the traditional pink for a girl, or blue for a boy, and hedge your bets by using lemon or turquoise to sew the soother, the card can be sewn well in advance and needs very little work to finish it after the birth is announced.

The Pattern Library may give you inspiration for other cards. For example, to thank a midwife or a nurse after a stay in hospital, you will find the figure of a nurse, and the words THANK YOU are drawn out in Fig 55. Any figure that resembles the person receiving the card, together with a brief message, will make a card that will be kept when others are discarded. This chapter has offered many suggestions, but no doubt you will have your own ideas.

MOUNTING YOUR WORK INTO A CARD
If you want to avoid having to make your own card mount, use one of the many ready-made mounts that are available for the display of pressed flowers, lace or embroidery. Buy your card mount first and use the calculations in Chapter 2 to ensure that your embroidery will fit the card 'frame' before you start to design and sew. Press your work as described in Chapter 12. Spread adhesive evenly over sections A and B of the card (Fig 56). Position your embroidery face down on section B, ensuring that it is not crooked; fold A over B and stick down firmly, thus sandwiching your embroidery between A and B (Fig 57). Alternatively, you can mount your work into the card using lengths of double-sided sticky tape. If you use an aerosol adhesive, as described in Chapter 1, mask section C with a piece of paper whilst you apply the adhesive to sections A and B.

If you opt to make your own card mount, you are free to produce a design of any shape or size you wish. Use thin card, which can be any colour you choose and can complement the embroidery. Before cutting the card

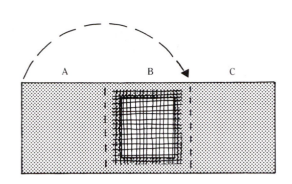

Fig 57 Folding the card

make a quick, rough mock-up in paper to check that the card will fit the embroidery. The window can be any shape you require: rectangular, square, round, oval, heart shaped etc, but do not attempt to cut it out with scissors; for a professional finish use a sharp craft knife both to cut away the window opening and to score the fold lines. Proceed as described above to mount your work into your card. Lastly, be sure to use your best handwriting inside the card.

USING AN EMBROIDERY HOOP AS A MOUNT
The greeting WELCOME TO YOUR NEW HOME has been mounted onto an embroidery hoop, instead of into a card (Plate 15), so that it can be hung on the wall for display. This method of mounting can be used for any design, and is an appropriate finishing touch as the work may have been produced on the very hoop which is being used as a mount. However, because the work is not held behind glass it has no protection from dust and grime.

Use a hoop that is not much larger than the design you have sewn. Bind the inner hoop with a white bias tape; this will not only protect the embroidery when it is mounted onto the hoop but will be a convenient anchorage for the stitching and lace that will neaten the raw edges of the work on the reverse. Press your work as described in Chapter 12. Tack a piece of plain, light-coloured cotton fabric onto the reverse side of your work, to serve as a lining which will hide the back of the stitching from view. Lay your work face up over the inner hoop and press the outer hoop down over it. Take great care to ensure that the screw adjuster is positioned centrally at the top; this is the point from which the work will be suspended, and if not correctly placed your work will hang at a drunken angle. Tighten the screw adjuster so that the work is held taut in the hoop. Trim away the excess fabric on the reverse, close to the hoop. If you are a perfectionist you will sew down the raw edges of the fabric to the cotton binding tape with buttonhole stitch; if not, use adhesive. Sew a length of white broderie anglaise lace to the cotton binding tape to hide any raw edges. Lacemakers could substitute a length of gathered hand-made lace to provide the finishing touch.

Fig 56 Making a mount for a greetings card

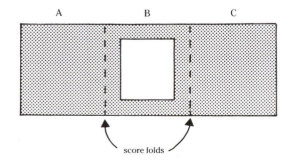

score folds

◁ *Fig 55 Alphabets 6 and 7. Names and greetings*

(overleaf) Plate 15

7 Texts

Many of us have a favourite text, be it from a poem, a hymn, a song or some other source, which we would like to embroider and hang on the wall. Those available as kits usually confine themselves to short sayings such as 'Home, Sweet Home', and the chances are that your favourite lines will not be available ready-charted. There are three texts in this chapter and the treatment of each is explained so that, even if the wording is not to your choice, you will be able to follow the same processes to produce a design for your own favourite lines. Three very different borders have been designed to cater for a variety of tastes and each can be filled with wording other than that suggested here.

'GATHER YE ROSEBUDS' (Plates 16 and 17)

Many old cross-stitch texts, of the 'Thou Shalt Not' variety, are of a stern, forbidding nature and a high moral tone. Preferring a positive exhortation to a negative one, the following lines by Robert Herrick have long been favourites of mine:

> Gather ye rosebuds while ye may,
> Old Time is still a-flying:
> And this same flower that smiles to-day,
> Tomorrow will be dying.

When starting to design a chart of a text, the first decision is whether to use a cross-stitch or a back-stitch alphabet for the lettering. Because the verse in this case is quite long, a back-stitch alphabet was used (Fig 54). If a cross-stitch alphabet had been used, the design would have been too large to fit the space where the finished embroidery was to hang.

The lettering was drawn out, each line being put on a separate strip of graph paper, ready to cut to size later. Next a border was chosen. The subject matter of a text can often suggest a suitable border to contain it, and in this case rosebuds were the obvious choice. These were drawn out to form a regular trellis pattern with an inner line representing a threaded ribbon tied in a bow at the top in the centre. The border could be filled with any text which fits, or could be expanded to take a longer text. Your choice of lines to fill this border can be on any subject, but here are more suggested texts with a floral theme:

> And I wove the thing to a random rhyme,
> For the Rose is Beauty, the Gardener, Time.
> (Austin Dobson)

> Each Morn a thousand Roses brings, you say:
> Yes, but where leaves the Rose of Yesterday?
> (Edward Fitzgerald)

> And I will make thee beds of roses
> And a thousand fragrant posies.
> (Christopher Marlowe)

> One thing is certain, that Life flies;
> One thing is certain, and the Rest is Lies;
> The Flower that once has blown for ever dies.
> (Edward Fitzgerald)

> Full many a flower is born to blush unseen,
> And waste its sweetness on the desert air.
> (Thomas Gray)

> Flowers of all hue, and without thorn the rose.
> (John Milton)

With the text chosen, the wording drawn onto strips of graph paper and the border copied out, the lettering was fitted inside the border. As the line 'And this same flower that smiles to-day', is so much longer than the others, it had to be split in two. When splitting a line, take some heed of the sense and split it at an appropriate point. In this case the split was made to read as 'And this same flower/that smiles to-day' which is a more natural break than 'And this same flower that/smiles to-day'. When you have positioned your lettering inside the border check that you are happy with the spacing between letters, between words, and between lines. If you decide you need larger spaces there is no need to erase your work and re-draw it. Simply cut your strip of lettering at the appropriate point and paste in some extra graph paper to enlarge the space. If spaces are too generous, again cut the strip at the appropriate point and overlap the cut edges to narrow the gap. Check that your lettering is not too close to the border at any point.

When the lettering is in position there may be spaces which would look better filled with a decorative symbol. When deciding how to fill any gaps, go back to the sense of the lines. In this case the poet talks of rosebuds, roses in full bloom and dead roses. The rosebuds have already appeared in the border, so roses in full bloom were used to fill the gaps at the end of lines 2 and 3. Dead roses were not very inspiring, but they are followed by rose-hips which are decorative, so these were chosen to fill the last two gaps. The life cycle of the rose is thus pictorially represented to echo the sense of the lines.

Fig 58 Cross-stitch alphabet for texts

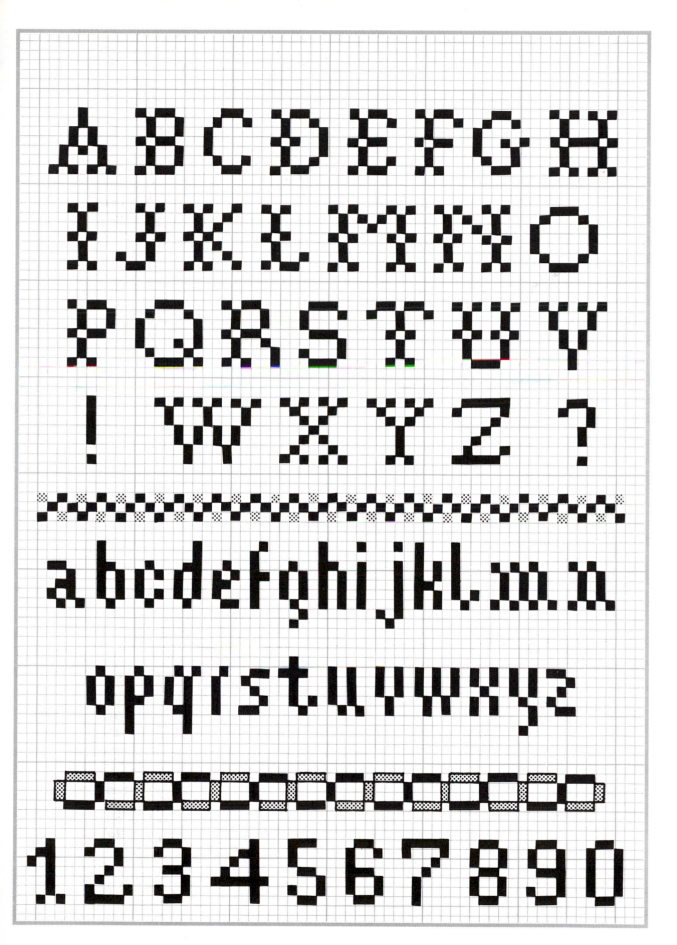

Gather ye rosebuds while ye may,

Old Time is still a-flying:

And this same flower that smiles today,

Tomorrow will be dying.

ROBERT HERRICK

ACCEPT THIS TRIFLE (Fig 59 and Plate 12)

Accept this trifle from a friend
Whose love for you will never end.

This is a traditional verse, taken from an old Welsh sampler, which should not take too long to sew and can be given as a gift, or to accompany one.

Because the verse is so short it was possible to use a cross-stitch alphabet (Fig 58) and still have a small design. The wording was drawn out onto long strips of graph paper which were cut to size when the border was in position. The border is a simple one which intertwines in a 'friendly' manner at the corners to echo the sentiment of the verse. This border is easily adjusted to fit any length of text. So, if you want to add extra wording such as 'From . . . To . . .', and the date, simply extend the parallel lines between the corners to the desired length.

The strips of lettering were cut to size, each line being broken at a natural point. They were then shuffled around on the master sheet to get a pleasing arrangement. Gaps were filled with tiny hearts and flowers. The flower in the top line was inserted towards the middle of the line, rather than placed at the end, to prevent repetition of the flower at the end of the bottom line.

If this design is embroidered onto a fine Aida or even-weave fabric, the result can be mounted into a card (Plate 12). If worked onto Hardanger or a coarse evenweave fabric it can be mounted into a more durable frame.

'THE THINGS I SOW' (Plates 18 and 19)

The things I sow
Somehow don't grow,
I'm sorely disenchanted –
But, oh, what luck
I have with stuff
I never even planted.

This verse might strike a chord with gardeners and appeared in a gardening magazine, authorship unknown. Because of the length of the verse, and the decision to design on a small scale, a back-stitch alphabet was chosen for the lettering. Once again the lettering was drawn out onto long strips of graph paper which were cut to size and placed in their approximate positions on the master sheet. Taking its cue from the sense of the verse, the border of wild flowers was assembled around the lines of lettering. The plants were traced from botanical books onto graphed tracing paper, were squared-up and cut out separately. They were placed on the master sheet, were shuffled around and plants were overlapped to get a rectangular shape that fitted with the lettering. In addition to the flora some fauna crept in to fill the odd awkward gap. This border is in complete contrast to the rosebud border, but still allows you to substitute your own text.

To expand the border horizontally, when you have copied it out onto graph paper, make a cut to the left of the daisy and ferns at the bottom. Cut between the butterfly and ivy at the top, to separate the left-hand side of the border from the right. Insert extra graph paper to get the size you require and fill the gaps with an extra leaf or two.

To expand the border vertically, give all the plants longer stalks, but take care not to distort the balance of the composition. In this way longer texts can be inserted.

The following texts are suggested as alternatives:

The kiss of the sun for pardon,
The song of the birds for mirth,
One is nearer God's Heart in a garden
Than anywhere else on earth.

(Dorothy Gurney)

God Almighty first planted a garden; and, indeed, it is the purest of human pleasures.   (Francis Bacon)

A garden is a lovesome thing, God wot!   (T. E. Brown)

To me the meanest flower that blows can give
Thoughts that do often lie too deep for tears.

(William Wordsworth)

Whatsoever a man soweth, that shall he also reap.

(Galatians 6: 7)

To see a World in a grain of sand,
And a Heaven in a wild flower,
Hold Infinity in the palm of your hand,
And Eternity in an hour.

(William Blake)

Or perhaps you have your own ideas.

OTHER SUGGESTIONS

All things bright and beautiful,
All creatures great and small,
All things wise and wonderful,
The Lord God made them all.

(C. F. Alexander)

The Pattern Library contains many ideas for a verse such as this. There are 'bright' butterflies, 'beautiful' flowers, a 'great' horse, 'small' mice, a 'wise' owl and 'wonderful' bees. The whole could be surrounded with a border of flowers or one made up of animal life.

How doth the little busy bee
Improve each shining hour,
And gather honey all the day
From every opening flower!

(Isaac Watts)

Once again, the Pattern Library has patterns of bees and a beehive, and throughout the book there are floral borders to choose from. To sum up, first choose your text and decide whether to use a back-stitch or a cross-stitch alphabet to draw out the lettering onto strips of graph paper. Cut the lettering strips to size and fit them into your chosen border. Try to fill any large gaps with a symbol that has some relevance to the meaning of the text. Lastly, give credit where it is due and include the name of the author of your text in your design.

Fig 59 Chart for text, illustrated in colour in Plate 12 ▷
(overleaf) Plate 18 and Plate 19 'The Things I Sow'

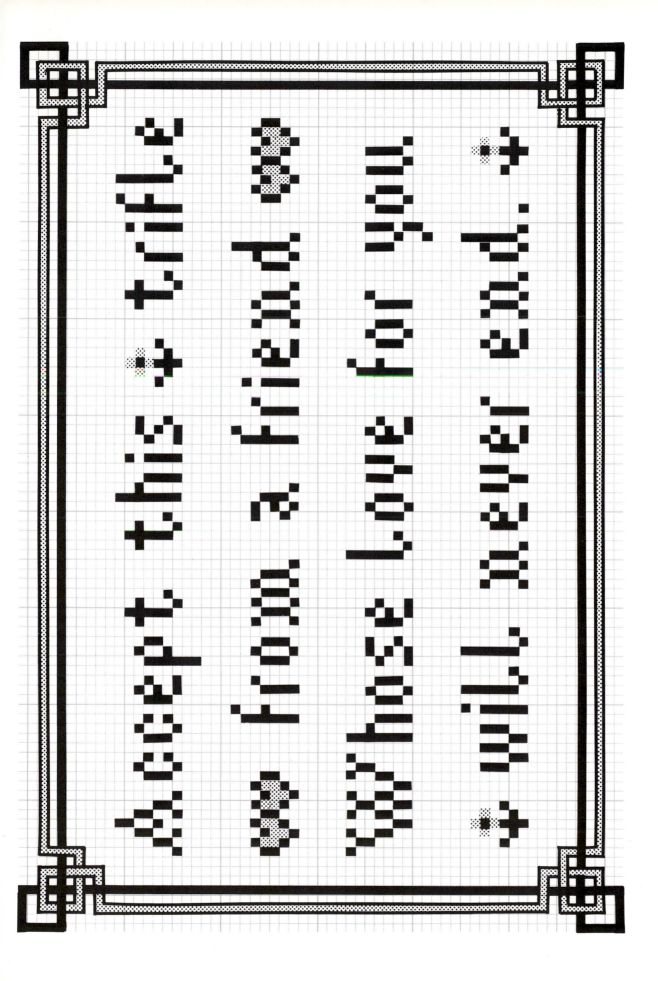

The things I sow
Somehow don't grow.
I'm sorely disenchanted —
But, oh, what luck
I have with stuff
I never even planted.

8 House and Family Samplers

During the eighteenth and nineteenth centuries many samplers were worked by young people as classroom exercises to teach them the art of needlework. A large number survive to this day in museums and private collections, or as heirlooms passed down through generations of the same family. All are highly valued and of interest both to needleworkers and those who study social history, giving a glimpse into life as it was lived in those days. A typical sampler design consisted of a floral border inside which were stitched an alphabet and numbers, reflecting life in the classroom. Often a house was represented which may have been the home of the embroiderer or some local landmark. Animals, flowers and other traditional symbols, each with a meaning, were often included, together with a motto or verse of high moral tone.

YOUR HOUSE AND FAMILY

Embroidering a house and family sampler today gives an opportunity to make not only a statement about your family, your home and the life led in it, but also to make your record in a contemporary style which will be of interest to future generations. Many kits and patterns are available for you to sew, but they are generally based on old sampler designs which have been worked many times before and so have nothing new to say. The time involved in sewing a kit and in sewing your own design will be the same, but the satisfaction of producing a unique piece of work for posterity will be far greater than that derived from producing a copy of someone else's work. To make a truly personal and up-to-date statement you will have to undertake the design work yourself and this chapter offers step by step instructions. As everybody's life is different, follow the processes used in the production of the design for the sampler of my childhood home (Plate 23) and then adapt them to your own circumstances. Before starting, make sure you have read the general design instructions in Chapter 2.

First make a list of ingredients, ie a list of everything you would like to record in your design, under the following suggested headings:

House	your present or a previous home
Family	immediate or extended family
Pets	the more the merrier
Garden	assorted flora and fauna
Location	town, county or area where the house is situated
Nationalities	countries of origin of family members, or which have influenced family life
Work	the occupations of family members
Interests	hobbies and pastimes
Alphabet and numbers	
Border	

Your list needs to be flexible as some items may not fit, or may not be suitable for some other reason, in which case it is better to save discarded material for another occasion rather than try to cram everything in willy-nilly.

The house

Even if it is not a thing of great architectural beauty, the family home is an important part of our lives and deserves to be made the focal point of a house and family sampler. Unless you live in Buckingham Palace or the White House, you are not likely to find a ready-made chart of your home and you will have to draw it onto graph paper yourself. A watercolour painting of my home (Plate 22) was used as the basis of my design, but a photograph or sketch would have done just as well. As the painting was conveniently the size needed for the design, a piece of graphed tracing paper was placed over the watercolour, lining up as many vertical and horizontal lines as possible before starting to trace. The tracing of the house was squared-up as described in Chapter 2. Absolute accuracy was not possible in this medium, but when the house looked recognisably like home it was copied from the graphed tracing paper onto ordinary graph paper. Next it was coloured in with crayons, then cut out and put to one side to await the rest of the list of ingredients.

If you have no painting or photograph from which to work, you will need to make a sketch of your house. This is not as daunting as it sounds when you realise that most houses consist of straight lines which make them easy to draw. Stand square-on in front of the house and, to avoid as many awkward angles as possible, draw only one plane of the house. Be prepared for curious stares from passers-by as you do this. When you have a sketch

Fig 60 Charted houses

showing all the detail you wish to include and with the windows, doors, walls and roof correctly spaced in relation to each other, go indoors to put your sketch onto graph paper. If the picture, photograph or sketch that you are working from is the size you want for the finished design, it can be traced directly onto graphed tracing paper or graph paper. If it is too large or too small it can be enlarged or reduced as described in Chapter 2. If you do not want to go to this trouble, or if you have no graphed tracing paper, simply draw the house to the size you want straight onto the graph paper referring to your sketch or photo to help you. The next step is to square-up the drawing or tracing of the house as described in Chapter 2.

Doors When squaring-up, start with the door. Find the smallest detail you want to show; you may have a much-prized door knocker so you will have to allow at least one square for this and draw the door around it to the correct proportions. Remember, the more detail you want to include, the larger your design will have to be. The size can be kept down if details such as door knockers, handles, letter-boxes etc can be later sewn in back stitch and French knots. Examples of doors can be found on Plate 20 and they appear in embroideries throughout this book.

When you have drawn your door you can add the porch, if you have one, and then proceed to draw in the windows, getting the proportions and spacing between them as accurate as the graph paper allows.

◁ *Plate 20*

Plate 21 'Apple End'. A house in the woods, hence the border of leaves and woodland creatures. The owners' initials have been included, also their cats, and an apple core to represent the name of the house

Windows Depending on the size of your design, you can allow one line of squares for glazing bars between panes of glass, or, if this makes your windows too large, draw the glazing bars in as back-stitch lines. Back stitch can also be used to suggest leaded lights. Circular windows can be drawn using a combination of full and three-quarter cross stitch. Curtains and blinds are easily added, pot plants and cats can sit on window sills and all help to make the house recognisable (Plate 20). Look carefully at your windows and see which details can be added to make it look more like home. With the door and windows in place you can now draw in the side walls and the ground line. Keep checking to ensure that the proportions and spacing look right.

Roofs Your house now needs a roof. Roofs in cross-stitch embroidery can rise straight up in two parallel lines, or in a series of small steps converging towards the top. A gentler slope can be achieved by using the off-setting technique described in Chapter 2. Roofs can also rise at an angle of 45° if three-quarter cross stitch is used. Study the roofs in this chapter and throughout the book, and choose whichever method best suits your house. Thatch can be suggested by the use of colour and back-stitch detail, as can slates or tiles. Do not forget to add the chimney, if you have one.

With the basic house drawn you can now add other details that make it look like home. Window boxes, tubs of flowers, hanging baskets, lanterns and steps are just a few details that help to distinguish your home from your neighbour's, especially if you live in a row of houses all built to the same design. Indicate back stitch and French knots on your chart for small details and climbing plants. Draw out the name of the house if you plan to include it. For extra help refer to Fig 60 (houses), Plate 20 (doors, windows etc) and Plates 58 and 59 (gardens).

As each design on your list is completed, colour it in, cut it out and put it in an envelope for safe keeping until you are ready to arrange all your ingredients on the master sheet.

The family
Family members can appear as figures taken from the Family page of the Pattern Library, or can be figures dressed in clothes to indicate their occupations. The latter was the approach chosen for the design of my own family. To represent my father, the figure of the hospital doctor in the Pattern Library was turned into a family doctor by changing the white coat for a suit (Fig 61). My mother was a nurse and the figure in the Pattern Library needed no alteration. My sister appears in her school uniform, and is the basic female figure with the addition of a school pill-box hat, blazer and pleated skirt. The figure in the teacher's academic cap and gown, to represent me, was taken from Plate 14.

The Pattern Library may have just the figure you want, or you may be able to alter one of the figures to suit your needs; further instructions for altering figures are given in the Pattern Library. Alternatively, family names can be used instead of figures. Accompany each name with a relevant symbol, as was done in 'The Old Vicarage' sampler (Plate 27). If this is the method you prefer, first choose the alphabet you are going to use for the names. Draw out the names onto strips of graph paper; then draw out an appropriate symbol from the Pattern Library to accompany each name.

Pets
My cat and her kittens were taken from the Pattern Library and coloured appropriately. The rabbits, budgerigar and ducks came from the same source. Because we had a large number of kittens and rabbits, one kitten and one rabbit have been given a different pose to add variety to the line-up.

There are many different animals and breeds of animals in the Pattern Library so hopefully you will find your pet there. If not, follow the instructions in the Pattern Library to create your own animal design.

Garden
Apple blossom and butterflies were used to form my border, and other garden flowers were drawn out as small bands of flowers. The squirrels and the owls which lived in the trees in the garden have been taken from the Pattern Library, where there is a complete section on gardens. The garden picture (Plate 25) may provide you with further inspiration.

Location
The county of Herefordshire has been represented in my sampler by cider apples and a jar of cider. The Hereford bull was adapted from the bull in the Pattern Library. You might choose to show the location of your house by means of a local landmark, in which case postcards are helpful. 'The Old Vicarage' sampler (Plate 27) shows a statue of Lady Godiva with the three spires, to represent Coventry; the pavilion in the Jephson Gardens which represents Leamington Spa; and the clock tower in Kenilworth.

Nationalities
My family connections with Canada, Ireland and Wales are represented by the maple leaf, the shamrock and the leek, all taken yet again from the Pattern Library. The French and Spanish flags represent my previous occupation as a language teacher. Consult Plates 50 and 51 for further help.

Work
The occupations of my family members were portrayed by dressing the family in the clothing appropriate to the occupation of each person, and in the case of my father by also making him carry the tools of the trade. The serpent twining around the staff was included as an extra medical symbol for my parents' professions, and also because there was an awkward gap to fill and the symbol balanced well in shape and colour with the leek.

Many occupations can be found in the Pattern Library as figures dressed for work. Perhaps your chosen occupation has no distinctive clothing associated with it, or maybe you have already used figures from the Family page of the Pattern Library, or you do not want to use figures at all. Instead, you can use the tools of the trade, or even the place of work, to represent an occupation. Search the Pattern Library for designs that suit your circumstances.

Interests
Raid the Pattern Library for symbols to represent the interests and hobbies on your list of ingredients. For some subjects there is more than one alternative from which to choose, and your choice will depend on the prominence you want to give the symbol and on the space available. For example, a piano could have been chosen to represent 'music' on my sampler, but as all the other symbols in this section of the sampler were small, the piano would have been rather large with no other symbol of comparable size to balance with it. Instead some bars of music were chosen.

Alphabet and numbers
The inclusion of an alphabet and numbers provides a link with the old tradition of sampler making. Because of the age of the house in my sampler a traditional alphabet was chosen (Fig 63); a more modern house might look better if an alphabet which includes three-quarter cross stitch were used. Both upper case and lower case alphabets are traditionally sewn on samplers, but if you do not have room for both, use the upper case, ie capital letters. Draw out your chosen alphabet onto long strips of graph paper which will be cut to size later. Add a few small flowers

Fig 61 How to change a figure. Copy out the figure closest to your needs (a), erase those features you do not want (b), draw in the new details which may be taken from another figure (c), colour and cut out your new figure (d). Here a hospital doctor has been transformed into a family doctor

and hearts to the end of the strips; these will be used later to fill any gaps which are left when the alphabet is fitted inside the border. Draw out the numbers from 1 to 10; you may not have room for them all when you come to the assembly stage, or you may need to draw out more later.

Border
The size of my sampler design allowed me to use quite a wide border, and an inner and outer black retaining line were added to match the black timbers on the house. The colours in the border should echo the colours used somewhere in the central design. Both the apple blossom and the butterflies are in the Pattern Library.

When choosing a border for your design you might like to make it personal in some way. The name of the house or the street it is in might suggest a theme, eg Beehive Hill, Cherry Cottage. Perhaps a border could be formed from a symbol on your list or you could use a favourite flower. Whatever you choose, follow the instructions on borders in Chapter 2 and draw out your pattern onto four long strips of graph paper, approximately to the length you think you will need.

At this stage your envelope should be bulging with drawings, each coloured in and cut out neatly. You are now ready to start arranging them on your master sheet.

Assembling the chart
Fig 62 shows some of the common errors easily made at this stage and demonstrates how NOT to arrange your design material on your master sheet. Compare it with the finished sampler (Plate 23) and note the following mistakes.
- The design material has been arranged to make a tall, 'portrait' shaped picture, but because the house is wider than it is tall, a wide, 'landscape' shape would be more suitable.

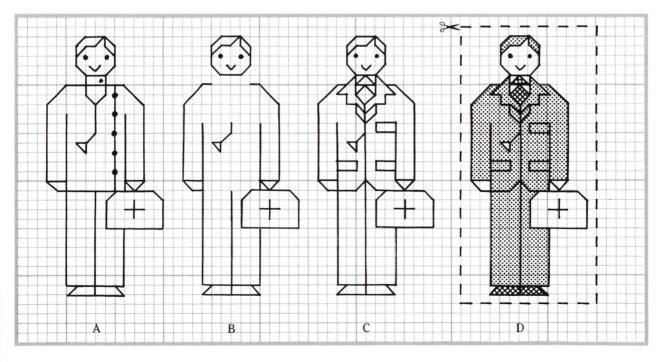

A   B   C   D

Plate 22 Watercolour of my childhood home, painted by Helen Lodge

Plate 23 Sampler 'My Childhood Home' ▷

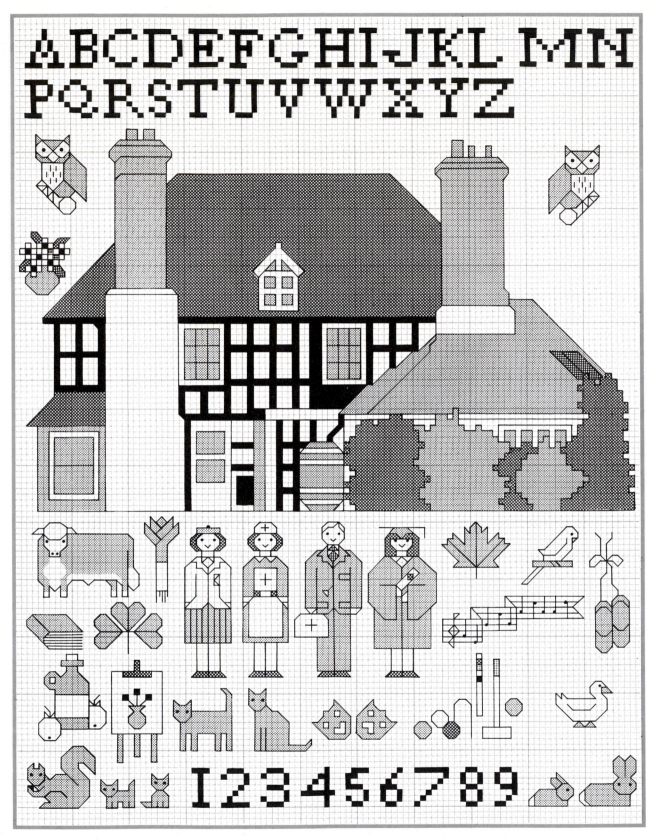

*Fig 62 How **not** to arrange your design material*

- The house has been positioned too high up making the design top heavy. It is better to have the house about two-thirds of the way down and, if anything, for the design to err on the side of being bottom heavy.
- Check the alphabet; a letter has been left out which is easily done, and the spacing between the 'L' and the 'M' could be improved. The second line of the lettering needs to be centred; or the gap after the 'Z' needs filling with hearts or flowers.
- All the animals are facing out of the picture. If they were reversed the eye would be drawn inwards. The kittens have been squeezed in beside the squirrel but they belong more logically with the cats.
- The two owls have been positioned carelessly, one is a fraction lower than the other.
- The rest of the design material has been crammed into the remaining space in a disorganised manner. The design does not balance well from right to left, the left side being more crowded than the right. The vase of flowers has been stuck in as an afterthought and has no symbol to balance it on the other side.
- The flags which were on my list of ingredients are missing; it is all too easy for drawings to disappear without trace into the vacuum cleaner if they are not put into an envelope for safe keeping as work progresses.

In the final version you will see that the design has been made 'landscape' shaped and that the house has been moved down. A larger master sheet was used to make the design less cramped and the extra space has been filled with additional material. Separate areas of interest have been created by the use of a twisting ribbon and bands of flowers to organise the design material into different categories – family, pets, interests etc.

When arranging your design material, the most usual way is to put your alphabet and numbers at the top of the design with your house centrally two-thirds of the way down, and arrange the rest of the material in the remaining available space. But you may have your own unique formula, so try many different layouts until you find one which pleases you. It does not matter what anyone else thinks. This is your own statement, nobody else's. Because the ingredients of the design are each on a separate piece of paper, you can shuffle them around as much as you like without having to erase and re-draw them every time you change your mind. In this way you can satisfy yourself that you have tried many different arrangements and you will not have to wonder for years to come if the cat would have looked better beside the dog instead of beside the budgerigar. You might prefer to place all symbols referring to one person with that person, as was done in 'The Old Vicarage' sampler, or have a more general arrangement.

At this stage be prepared to be flexible; discard any material which is causing problems because of size or unsuitability. Ask yourself if everything balances well; is one side fuller than the other? Is the whole design top heavy? Are there any gaps which need filling? Go back to your list of ingredients and see if there is anything else you can add; often a flower or two, or a heart, are sufficient to

fill a gap. Do not over-clutter the design; look at the spaces you have left around the drawings as well as looking at the drawings themselves. Do areas of the design need separating from each other by means of a small band of flowers or a twisted ribbon? This can have the effect of organising the symbols into separate defined areas, rather than just a hotchpotch of symbols floating around in space. Would your numbers look better at the bottom of the design? Try moving them and see what you think. Check your alphabet for mistakes. Are all your designs facing in the right direction to draw the eye inwards towards the focal point of your picture? Animals, vehicles, or anything which is not designed 'face on', should be pointed towards the centre of the design rather than the border. Otherwise they will look as if they are trying to escape from the picture. To reverse the direction of a design, hold a small hand mirror beside it and copy out the mirror image. Is your border correctly positioned around the design? Check the corners; does the border join up correctly? Have you left sufficient space between the border and the alphabet? Do any other drawings come too close to the border?

When you are satisfied with your arrangement, stick each drawing onto the master sheet taking care to match up the squares on the master sheet with the squares on your drawings. Pin the finished 'masterpiece' up on the wall, in a spot where you will see it frequently, and live with it for a few days. If you want to change anything, it is easier to do it at this stage than once you have started sewing. When you have lived with the design happily for a week, it is safe to start sewing.

When the work is finished, sign and date it for the benefit of future generations who will have great fun deciphering all your symbols. If these are very obscure, write out an explanation which can be stuck to the back of the frame to put the curious out of their misery.

'MY GARDEN' PICTURE
Keen gardeners may be more inspired to immortalise their plot than their house. When designing the chart for my own garden (Plate 24) full use was made of artistic licence whilst still aiming for a faithful record. Normal perspective was mixed with a 'bird's eye' view and no regard was taken of the seasons so that all the plants are shown in full bloom at the same time. No photographic record could have been so flexible.

The border was made up of all the different types of fencing and walling surrounding the garden, with an abstract pattern at the top where the fencing ended. At the top of the picture is the back of the house showing the kitchen window with its blind and two plants inside the kitchen. Under the window is a window box. The dining room window has four pot plants on the window sill and is surrounded by a wistaria. To the left of the house is a trellis supporting honeysuckle. The paved patio has tubs of geraniums and nasturtiums and is bordered by a rockery, represented by a single band of small flowers. Stepping stones lead across the lawn to a greenhouse which is full of morning glory flowers, coleus and tomatoes, the latter worked in large French knots to add

'Il faut cultiver notre jardin'

Plate 24 Chart for 'My Garden' (see page 65)

Plate 25 'My Gard

texture and variety to the picture. A magnolia tree is in full bloom behind the greenhouse, and to the right is a pampas grass, beside a rustic arch on which are growing climbing roses and clematis. The shrub beside the arch is a winter-flowering viburnum and on the far right are a flowering red currant and forsythia.

The vegetable plot, from top to bottom, shows cabbages worked in bullion bars, strawberries, peas (French knots), asparagus (back stitch), lettuces (bullion bars), radishes, cauliflowers (bullion bars and French knots), raspberries (one unripened to relieve the monotony), carrots and runner beans (Plate 7). On the other side is a herbaceous border with lupins, oriental poppies, daisies, hollyhocks, delphiniums and other perennials. Butterflies commonly seen in the garden have been worked into the four corners, a cabbage white naturally being chosen for the vegetable corner.

The large expanse of grass was rather daunting to sew, so it was broken up by scattering onto it as many different items as possible. The family cat was an obvious choice, as were birds and small butterflies around the plum and pear trees. The wheelbarrow, deck-chair and toys gave some indication of activities which take place in the garden. Finally the grass was striped as if it had just been mown, and the lawn-mower is shown with the job nearly completed, which allowed a further contrast of darker grass full of the inevitable daisies and dandelions. The quotation was taken from *Candide* by Voltaire.

By comparing the chart with the finished embroidery (Plate 25) you will notice that changes have been made as the work progressed. For example, square geraniums became round ones; carrots were added for an extra splash of colour and because boredom had set in with the production of the raspberries, showing that you can change your mind on some details right up until the day you take your work to be framed.

Fig 63 Traditional sampler alphabet

Plate 26 House and family sampler, a cryptic yet detailed record of family life

Plate 27 Sampler, 'The Old Vicarage' (sources, page 127). The pattern of the wrought iron in the front of the house has been used to form the border

9 Family Trees

One of the commonest symbols to be found on old samplers is the tree. Representing life, strength and fruitfulness, it appears in many stylized forms and has been revered by many cultures. The Tree of Knowledge bearing apples in the Garden of Eden, flanked by Adam and Eve, with the serpent twined around the trunk can be adapted to depict your family tree and can be surrounded by many symbols each with its own traditional meaning (Fig 64). It can symbolise our common ancestry, whilst the Oak Tree can represent the strength of family bonds. Patterns of both a Tree of Knowledge (Plate 28) and an Oak Tree (Fig 65) appear in this chapter.

TRADITIONAL SYMBOLS AND THEIR MEANINGS

Basket of fruit	fruitfulness and fertility
Dog	fidelity
Two doves facing each other	concord
Dove with an olive branch	peace and charity
Owl	wisdom
Peacock	vanity, luxury and ostentation
Bee	hope and industriousness
Hour glass	the perishableness of life
Anchor	steadfastness
Swan	the bird of love
Rose	the flower of love
Heart	love
Squirrel	mischief
Butterfly	joy, inconstancy
Bunch of grapes	Christ
Key	the key to the kingdom of Heaven
Candle	prayer
Beehive	monastic or other community

These are just a few that have been selected for patterns in this chapter (Fig 64). A more comprehensive list can be found in *Embroidery Motifs from Dutch Samplers* by Alberta Meulenbelt-Nieuwburg.

THE TREE OF KNOWLEDGE (Plate 28)

Adapting this pattern for your own Family Tree
No two families are the same, so to portray your own family the pattern given here will need some adjustment and rearrangement:

1   Read the general design instructions in Chapter 2. (As work progresses and each symbol is drawn out, colour it in, cut it out and store it in an envelope for safe keeping.)

2   On separate slips of graph paper write out the names of each family member using the alphabet of your choice. For long names choose a very tiny alphabet such as alphabet 5 (Fig 54). Add their dates of birth if you wish and have the space to do so.

3   Draw out one large apple per person.

4   Copy out the trunk of the tree with Adam and Eve on either side of it.

5   Copy out the cherubs and the crown, which represent a marriage made in Heaven.

6   Copy out several branches to fill any gaps between the names when you come to arrange them.

7   Copy out the pointed tree top.

8   Copy out two garlands and fill each with an appropriate initial from alphabet 6 (Fig 55). A garland symbolises eternal love, going round and round as it does without a break or an end.

9   Select from Fig 64 two traditional symbols which have some relevance to your family. Copy them out.

10   Copy out eight long apple and leaf border strips to the approximate size you think you will need, with eight large apples to go in the corners and in the centre of each side.

Take a sheet of graph paper large enough to hold the complete design (the master sheet), and lay out all your symbols on it. Place the tree trunk with Adam and Eve at the bottom, and start to place your apples and family names above them, arranging them with the oldest generation at the top and the youngest at the bottom. Space them out and build up a tree shape using the branches, and bits of trunk, to fill any gaps. Shuffle the apples, names and branches around until you are pleased with the arrangement. Try to have a name or two in the centre of the design to break up the line of the trunk above the height of Adam and Eve. If the addition of more apples would help to balance the design, but there are no family members to go with them, consider leaving blank spaces underneath them to be filled in at a later date as the family grows and newcomers arrive. Consider including an extra apple to carry the family surname. When the tree has been assembled, add the pointed tree top and place the crown at the top of the design. Position a cherub either side of the crown, and in the spaces beneath them put your two chosen traditional symbols. Depending on the shape of your tree you may have other gaps which can be filled with hearts, flowers, dates or other symbols.

Next place the garlands either side of Adam and Eve.

Fig 64 Traditional symbols

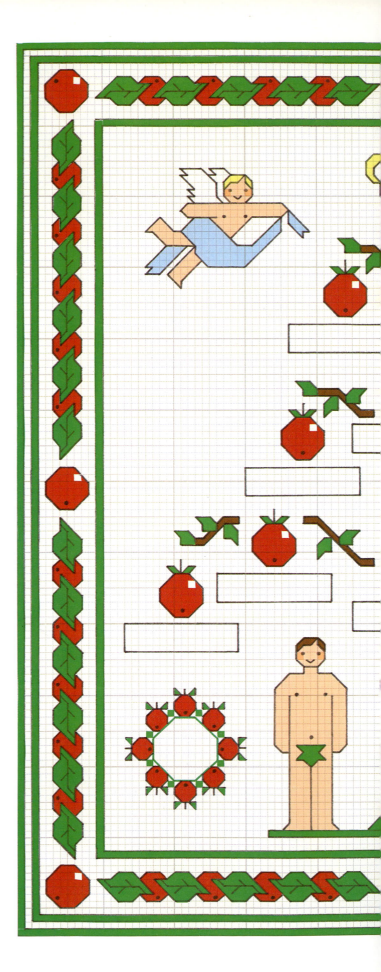

Plate 28 Chart for the Tree of Knowledge

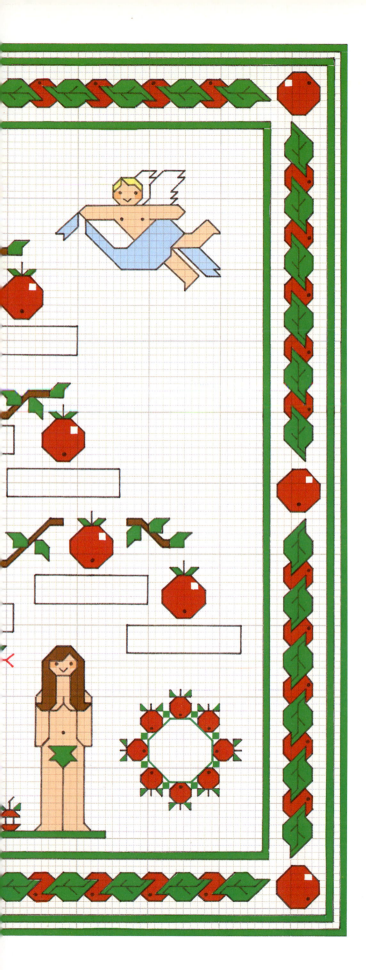

Fig 65 The Oak Tree chart

Position your eight border apples around the edge, one in each corner and one in the middle of each side, then lay your apple and leaf strips between them. If the border needs enlarging, lengthen the apple and leaf strips by adding more pattern repeats. If the strips are too long, shorten them by removing the necessary number of small apples and leaves. When you are happy with the spacing and arrangement of all the design material, draw an inner and outer retaining line around the border to complete the picture. Stick all the symbols down on to the master sheet, taking care to line up all the squares accurately. Pin your design on the wall and when you have lived with your design for a week and are happy with it, you are ready to start sewing.

Plate 30 shows how the basic pattern was adapted to produce a Family Tree for my husband's side of the family. An extra apple was added to allow the inclusion of the family surname and to fill a rather large gap in the centre of the tree. It was designed and embroidered to celebrate the Ruby Wedding Anniversary of my parents-in-law so some hearts and dates were added to fill gaps, and rich reds were used in the sewing to reflect the occasion.

THE OAK TREE (Fig 65)

Adapting this pattern for your own Family Tree

1   Read the general design instructions in Chapter 2. (As work progresses, colour in each symbol, cut it out and store it in an envelope for safe keeping.)
2   On separate slips of graph paper draw out the names of each family member using the alphabet of your choice. For long names choose a very tiny alphabet such as alphabet 5 (Fig 54). Add their dates of birth if you intend to use them and have room to do so.
3   Draw out one acorn per person.
4   Depending on the size of your proposed tree, draw out a number of oak leaves facing to the right and a number facing to the left.
5   Copy out the trunk of the tree, together with the toadstools, squirrel and badger. If you prefer other animals, substitute them. More animals can be found in the Pattern Library.
6   Draw out four long border strips of acorns and oak leaves to the approximate length you think you will need.

Take a sheet of graph paper large enough to hold the complete design (the master sheet), and lay all your symbols on it. Place the tree trunk and the animals at the bottom. Start to place the acorns and family names above the trunk, arranging them with the oldest generation at the top and the youngest at the bottom. Fill out the tree shape with oak leaves; those near the top of the tree should face upwards, those nearer the bottom need to be turned to face downwards. Leaves on the left-hand side of the tree should point to the left, and vice versa for those on the right. Similarly, turn the acorns to point in the right direction. Where one line of the family finishes and another continues, fill the gap with an owl or squirrel perched in the tree. Shuffle the names, acorns and leaves around until you are satisfied with the arrangement.

Lay your border strips around the edge of the design. If the border needs enlarging, add extra acorns and oak leaves to the strips. If the border needs reducing, cut off as many acorns and oak leaves as necessary. Check that you are happy with the arrangement of acorns or oak leaves in the four corners. Draw an inner and outer retaining line around the border to finish your design. Stick all your symbols onto the master sheet, taking care to line up the squares accurately. As previously recommended, live with your design on the wall for a week before you start to sew. Plate 29 shows how the Oak Tree pattern was used to produce a Family Tree for my side of the family.

Whether you choose the Oak Tree or the Tree of Knowledge, when you have sewn your design you will have a decorative and durable record of your family history.

Plate 29 Family Tree, adapted from the Oak Tree chart (Fig 65), to represent my side of the family

Plate 30 The Verso Family Tree, adapted from the Tree of Knowledge chart (Plate 28) to represent my husband's side of the family and to celebrate the Ruby Wedding Anniversary of my parents-in-law ▷

10 Marriage

Weddings, engagements and wedding anniversaries are all great family occasions to be recorded and celebrated in cross-stitch cards and pictures. In the wedding sampler (Plate 2), the approach is traditional and includes hearts, flowers and love birds, the only personalisation being the inclusion of names and a date. A more adventurous approach is possible by including, in addition, the figures of the people involved and the location.

A CHURCH WEDDING (Plates 31 and 34)

The basic chart records the marriage of the Duke and Duchess of York. A border of flowers and bows was designed. The bows were much favoured by the bride and, irrespective of this, they can represent 'tying the knot'. Wedding bells are included in the border at the top, and intertwined wedding rings are added at the bottom. Westminster Abbey is placed in the top, left-hand corner and is balanced by the wedding cake in the top right-hand corner. The bride, in her wedding dress, and the groom in his naval uniform, stand side by side in the church doorway. Either side stand the pages in their suits, and the bridesmaids carrying their hoops of flowers. The date is positioned at the top together with the name of the abbey and the time of the wedding. Two garlands, topped with a bow from the border, contain the bride and groom's initials. The bees and the thistle are taken from the bride's family coat-of-arms and the anchors represent the groom's naval career – the bride had all three embroidered onto the train of her dress so it was appropriate to include them. Small gaps are filled with rows of hearts.

Adapting the pattern for your own wedding

Before you begin, make sure you have read the general design instructions in Chapter 2. Unless you were married in Westminster Abbey, you should start by drawing out your own church, following much the same procedure as that given for drawing out a house. A photograph is useful, or visit the church and make a sketch. For more help with churches, turn to the section on Christenings in Chapter 11. Next draw out the wedding cake and give it the appropriate number of tiers. Add a large cakestand if you need extra height in order to get it to balance well with your church, or place a bottle of champagne and some glasses beside it to add extra width if necessary.

Next turn your attention to the bride. Use the basic bride figure from the Pattern Library; change the headdress, veil, hair style, dress and bouquet as necessary. Use back stitch and French knots for small details, but take care not to overdo their use or your figure will look cluttered. Choose the most important details and limit yourself to those rather than trying to add every last button and bead. A wedding photograph is a useful aid to memory for this. A figure of a groom can also be found in the Pattern Library; again, make any necessary changes or additions such as a beard, spectacles or whatever is needed to make him recognisable. If he wore a uniform, replace the morning suit with as accurate a uniform as possible. Stand the groom next to the bride and draw out the doorway of the church around them. If the doorway of your church differs greatly from the arch in the basic pattern you might choose to re-draw it. Bridesmaids and pages can be produced using the boy and girl figures in the Pattern Library, adding the appropriate clothing, or use the figures in this pattern as a starting point and make the necessary changes. The height of the figures can be adjusted to show differing ages amongst the children. The parents of the couple, the guests, the best man, the officiating priest, all can be drawn out and added to the line-up. Use figures from the Pattern Library, giving them recognisable clothing and headgear.

Using the alphabet of your choice, draw out the date of the wedding together with any other wording you wish to include. Copy out two garlands and fill each with an appropriate initial from alphabet 6 (Fig 55).

Draw out four long border strips, one containing the wedding bells for the top, one with wedding rings for the bottom and two side strips. Alternatively draw out another border of your choice.

Arrange all your symbols on the master sheet and shuffle them around to get the best arrangement. Figures can be positioned in one long line or in two, depending on their numbers. Whatever line-up you choose there will be gaps to fill with any symbols that have relevance to the couple. You may wish to make reference to their families, their work or their future life together. Look through the Pattern Library and see if there is anything you wish to include. If not, gaps can be filled with the garlands, any wording you have chosen, and small bands of hearts.

Position your border strips around the design. If you need a larger border than you at first thought, add extra pattern repeats; if you need a smaller border simply cut off the necessary number of repeats. When you are satisfied with the position of all your symbols, stick them down on to the master sheet and colour them in. The colour scheme of the border may be suggested by the colour of the bridesmaids' dresses, the bride's bouquet, or by colours worn by the guests. Link the colours in the border to a colour which has been used in the main picture.

Fig 66 Symbols for weddings, engagements and anniversaries

WESTMINSTER

23rd S

Plate 31 Chart, 'The Royal Wedding'
(see page 87)

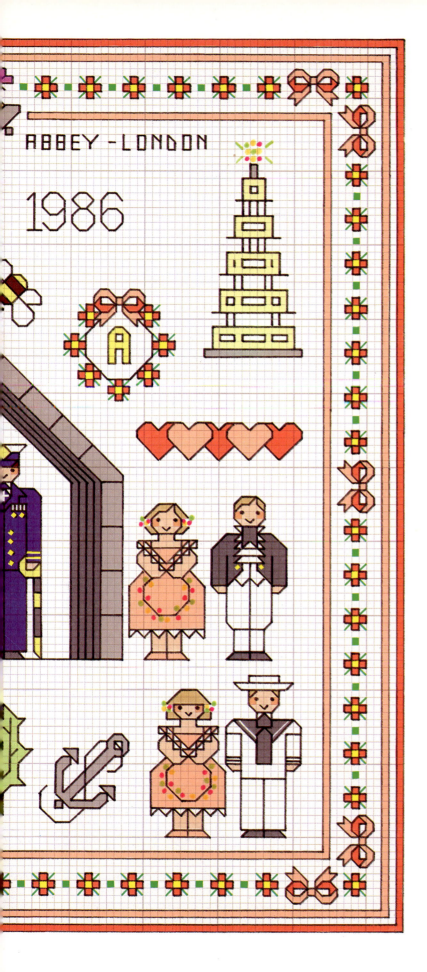

ABBEY -LONDON

1986

A

When adapting the basic pattern to suit my own wedding (Plate 33), the finished size of the design was reduced, as my wedding was a quieter affair with only two bridesmaids. The church was re-drawn from a postcard because the wedding photographs did not show the whole building. A champagne bottle and glasses were added beside the cake to make it balance in size with the church. The basic arch was used and the bride and groom were dressed appropriately. Guests appear dressed as they were for the wedding which took place in October, so the bridesmaids were dressed in autumn colours which are echoed in the border. The garlands were filled with our initials and the border was made smaller to fit the new design. Gaps were filled with bands of hearts and the two family names; lastly, horseshoes and white heather were included for luck.

A REGISTRY OFFICE WEDDING

Registry Office weddings have been sadly neglected by designers of cross-stitch patterns, but with a few changes of approach they can be celebrated in embroidery just as effectively as church weddings. The basic chart (Fig 67) has a romantic border of hearts and flowers, but as church bells would be inappropriate they have been replaced by two intertwined wedding rings. A standard porch entrance has been used instead of the arch of a church doorway. Space has been left above the door for you to include the name of the registry office where the wedding took place. The bride and groom stand side by side in the doorway and are dressed in their finery, as are their guests who stand either side. Space is left on both sides for the addition of the names of the couple. The date of the wedding is at the top together with two garlands for you to fill with appropriate initials. For good luck, horseshoes and white heather complete the picture.

Adapting this pattern for your own wedding

Following the basic design instructions in Chapter 2, begin by copying out the porch onto graph paper. You may be happy to use the basic porch pattern, but if the registry office in question has a distinctive entrance you may wish to re-draw it. A photograph is useful, or work from a sketch. Next copy out the bride and groom, together with any other figures you want to include in your design. Either use figures in this pattern as your starting point, or look through the Pattern Library to find more suitable ones, making changes to their clothing and appearance as necessary. Having chosen an appropriate alphabet, draw out the date and the names of the bride and groom. Copy out two garlands and fill each with an initial taken from alphabet 6 (Fig 55). Draw out four long border strips, remembering to include the rings at the top.

Put all your symbols on the master sheet and shuffle them around to find the best layout. If you have included more than six figures in your design, consider lining them up in two rows as in the Royal Wedding design. Position your border strips around the design and adjust them to

fit, checking that you have a pair of hearts correctly positioned in each corner. Fill any gaps with champagne bottles, horseshoes and heather, four-leaf clovers, rows of hearts or suitable symbols from the Pattern Library that have relevance to the couple. When you are happy with your design stick all your symbols to the master sheet to produce your chart for sewing.

In order to adapt the basic chart to record the wedding of friends (Plate 32), the porch was re-drawn from their wedding photograph. The entrance to this registry office is wide enough to accommodate the six figures required so they were all lined up inside the porch, the bride and groom standing on a step to give them prominence over the other figures. The bride wore a white coat and carried a muff, trimmed with flowers. She wore no hat, but pinned flowers in her hair. All these changes were made to the basic figure. The groom only needed the addition of a moustache, and the guests were drawn in the clothes they wore for the occasion. The name of the registry office appears in the doorway and there was just enough space to include the sprigs of white heather which, in view of the bride's name, Heather, were a 'must'.

ENGAGEMENTS

Having read through this chapter and those preceding it, you will see how a very personal record of an occasion can be put together. A greetings card offering congratulations to an engaged couple can be concocted from the designs of an engagement ring, champagne bottle and good luck symbols (Fig 66). The couple themselves could also be included using figures from the Pattern Library, and their occupations and interests may be found in the same source. A larger picture, such as the courtship picture (Plate 3) can be produced. Hearts, flowers, love birds, names, dates and figures are all grist to your mill and can be used to create a memorable and most acceptable gift.

WEDDING ANNIVERSARIES

Whether you are designing a card or a more ambitious picture, the designs in Fig 66 could be helpful. For a Silver Wedding consider using silver wedding-bells, silver horseshoes, a cake with the number 25 written on it, or even an enlarged cake with 25 candles. You may wish to represent the church where the couple were married or include symbols from the Pattern Library which are of relevance to the life they have lived together. For a Silver Wedding, use silver thread throughout your design where appropriate, and for a Golden Wedding, substitute gold thread. Ruby Weddings will require some use of red, in the border perhaps; the engagement ring (Fig 66) can become a ruby ring if sewn with ruby-coloured thread. Follow all the instructions on design previously given, to produce a unique piece of embroidery to celebrate the occasion.

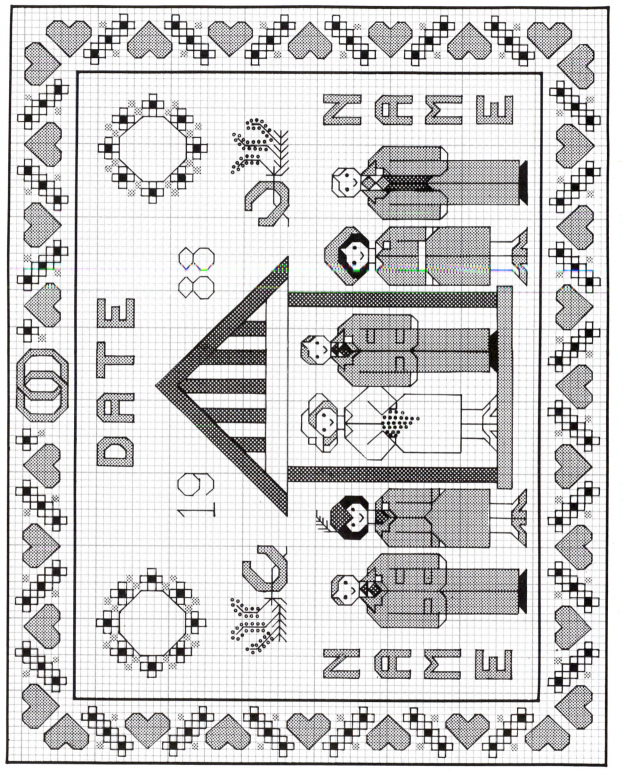

Fig 67 Chart for a Registry Office wedding

Plate 32 The wedding of friends, adapted from the Registry Office Wedding chart (Fig 67)

Plate 33 'My Wedding', adapted from the Royal Wedding chart (Plate 31)

Plate 34 'The Royal Wedding' ▷

11 Birth

What better excuse could there be to reach for your needle than the arrival of a new baby? A pattern for a birth announcement, a birth record, a christening and a nursery alphabet, all suitable for you to adapt, are included in this chapter.

BIRTH ANNOUNCEMENT
'The Rainbow Slide' (Fig 68)

A greetings card to welcome the arrival of a baby has already been given in the chapter on greetings cards. This design, if sewn onto a fine fabric, can also be mounted as a card (Plate 15), or if sewn on a fabric with a lower thread count will make a picture suitable for framing.

The chart announces the arrival of a baby and needs only the addition of the name and date to complete it. Sufficient space has been left for the addition of details such as weight, time of arrival etc, should you want to add them. The baby is sliding down to earth on a rainbow, and because of this unconventional method of arrival the design could also be suitable to announce the adoption of a baby. This idea is conveyed by the treasure in the crock of gold at the foot of the rainbow, and by the sun appearing from behind a cloud. Colour the stripes on the rainbow red, orange, yellow, green, blue, indigo and violet. For added realism the gold in the crock can be sewn using gold thread.

NURSERY ALPHABET (Plate 35)

This alphabet can be sewn without alteration, to make a cheerful decoration for a nursery wall. You may choose to add a simple retaining line or a border of your choice. Letters can be drawn out to spell a child's name or a single initial can be embroidered as a small gift. Change any or all of the colours if you wish, to suit a room's colour scheme or personal preferences.

CHRISTENINGS

As with the weddings in the previous chapter, a basic chart is provided for you to adapt to suit the christening you wish to record (Fig 69).

Adapting this pattern for your own circumstances

Before starting, read the general design instructions in Chapter 2. As work progresses colour in each symbol, cut it out and store it in an envelope for safe keeping until you are ready to assemble all the symbols on to your master sheet.

Begin with the church. You may either use the basic church pattern given here, or, if your church differs greatly, you may wish to re-draw it using a photograph or sketch to help. Pointed steeples present some difficulty as they do not rise at a convenient angle of 45°. If you feel that you have to include such a steeple, bring the pencil up the sides in a series of small steps. Check that both sides match and that both rise at the same pitch. Make use of the off-setting technique in Chapter 2 to soften the stepped effect. Remember that this is cross-stitch embroidery so allow yourself some artistic licence. If you want total accuracy you might be happier to work in another medium such as free-style embroidery or photography.

If you are not satisfied with your steeple, be prepared to be flexible; there are other approaches to representing a church. Perhaps it has a distinctive lich-gate or other feature which could be substituted, or maybe you could do a ground plan of the church seen from a bird's-eye view. If all else fails, consider drawing the altar with its linen and candlesticks. Whichever method you choose, the church can still be identified by drawing out its name in the lettering of your choice. If your church has a clock on the tower you can set the hands at the time the christening took place.

Copy out two floral crosses to place beside the church. Draw the font, or adapt it if your font differs greatly; add the two candles and then the water pouring from the shell. Copy out two white doves to place above the font. Using alphabet 3 (Fig 54), draw out the name of the baby and the date of the christening; the word 'Christened' can be replace with 'Baptised' if you prefer. Copy out the priest holding the baby and make any necessary adjustments to the appearance of the priest or to the christening robe that will make them more recognisable.

Draw out two parents and change their clothing and appearance to record how they looked on the day. Draw out the names of the godparents, putting a flower between each name. Copy out several bands of flowers which will be cut to size later to fill any gaps. Now draw out four border strips, each with a corner. If you have included more material than is given in the basic pattern, eg a larger church or more figures of guests around the font, lengthen the border strips by adding extra twists of ribbon at the points where the border reverses, not in the corners.

Arrange all your drawings on a master sheet and, using the basic pattern as a rough guide, shuffle them around to find the best arrangement. Fill any gaps with flowers, or remove flowers which have been squeezed out by the inclusion of extra design material. Check that your border fits correctly around the whole design, and when colouring it in use a light and a darker shade of the same colour to emphasise the twisting effect of the ribbon. The colour of the flowers in the border can be repeated in the floral crosses and bands of flowers. When you are satisfied with your layout, stick your symbols onto the master sheet with adhesive, to complete your chart.

When adapting the basic pattern to suit my own circumstances, both of my children were included in the design (Plate 36). Two sets of names and dates were used, so the lettering under the church was re-shuffled. Both babies had to make an appearance, so the figure of the priest holding the baby was reversed. This second priest figure was substituted for the parent figures. Two babies meant two sets of godparents, so again the lettering at the bottom needed some rearrangement. The newly created gaps were filled with flowers. The church was re-drawn in sufficient detail to make it recognisable and its name appears above it. When embroidering the water pouring from the shell into the font, silver thread was used to add sparkle to the occasion.

BIRTH RECORD

The picture of 'Harry' (Plate 37) has been designed as a birth record and includes all the details of his birth sewn onto his patchwork quilt. With a few simple changes the basic pattern (Fig 70) can be made to record the birth details of any baby.

Adapting this pattern for your own circumstances
1 Copy the outline shape of the bed onto graph paper. Decorate it with hearts and flowers.
2 Draw in the baby's head, adding more hair if desired; add the pillow and sheet.
3 Draw the squares on the quilt, but leave them blank for the time being.
4 Draw the potty and toys to be placed under and around the bed.
5 Using alphabet 6 (Fig 55) draw out the name of the

Fig 68 'The Rainbow Slide' chart

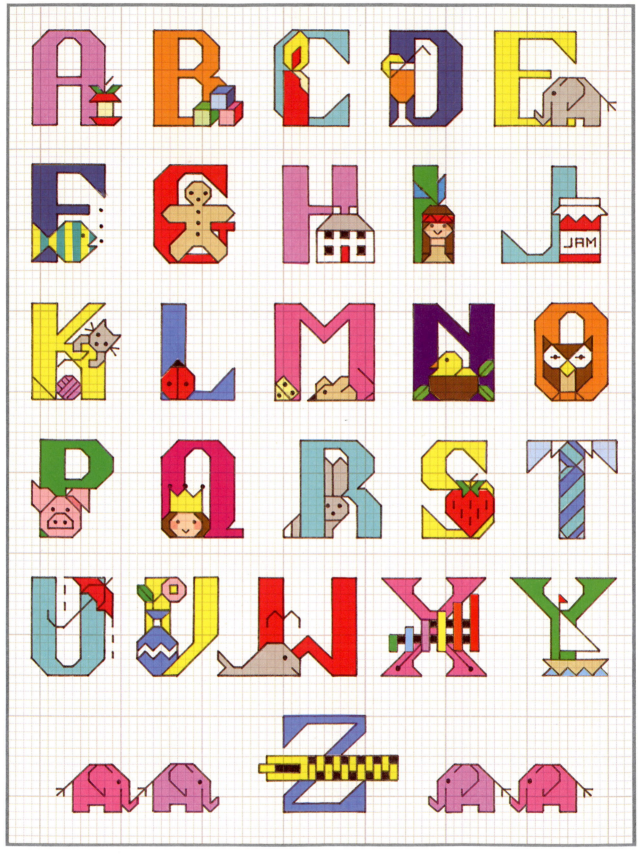

Plate 35 Nursery Alphabet

Plate 36 Baptismal record for my daughters, adapted from the christening chart (Fig 69) ▷

Fig 69 Chart for a christening

Fig 70 Chart for a birth record ▷

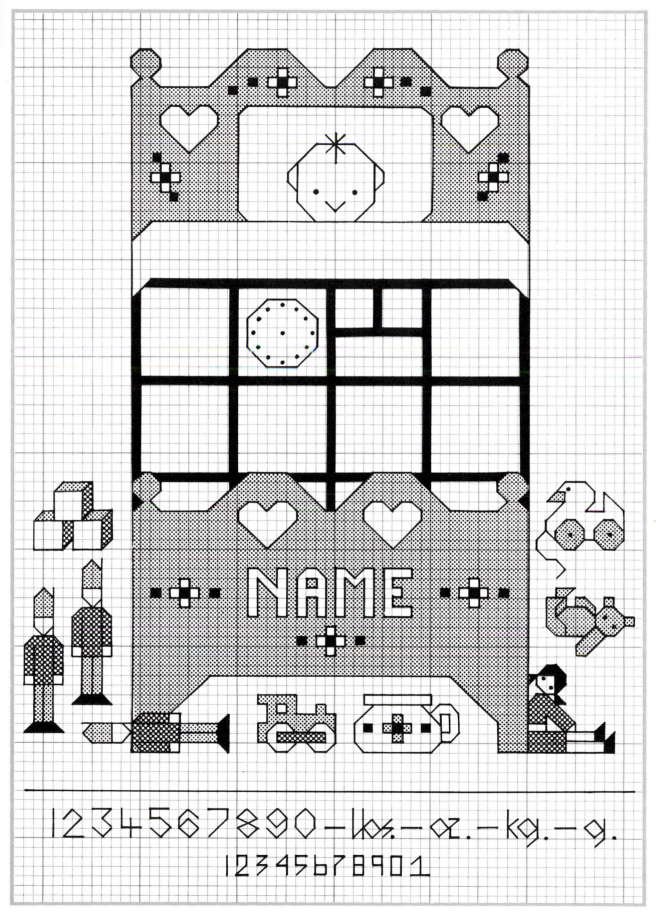

◁ Plate 37 'To Hilary from Ireland, and Joel from the U.S.A, a son, Harry, born at 2.30 p.m. on 21st July 1985 under the sign of Cancer, weighing 6lbs 6ozs.' A birth record for my nephew adapted from the birth record chart (Fig 70)

Plate 38 Birth record for my daughters (sources, page 127)

baby. If the name is too long to fit the space on the bed, dispense with the flowers either side of the name. If the name still does not fit in the space, choose a smaller alphabet, or one that can be sewn in back stitch. When you are satisfied with the name, stick it into place on the bed, taking care to centre it.

6 Fill the squares on the quilt with an appropriate symbol. Draw each symbol onto a separate piece of graph paper so that they can be shuffled around to find the best position for each one on the quilt.

Symbols to put on the quilt

Father's initial from alphabet 6 (Fig 55)

Clock to indicate the time of birth. Adjust the hands to show the correct time.

Date of birth

Mother's nationality. Use a small flag. Substitute the height of the baby at birth if you wish.

Weight at birth

Father's nationality. Use a small flag. Substitute the initial of a brother or sister if you wish.

Mother's initial from alphabet 6 (Fig 55)

Birth sign from the Pattern Library

Any small symbol that seems appropriate; a heart, a butterfly, a flower, can replace any of these suggestions.

Colour in your design to suit your taste, your colour scheme, or the sex of the baby, making the dominant colours pink for a girl or blue for a boy if you wish.

Arrange the drawings of the toys around the bed following the basic pattern, or in a new arrangement to suit yourself. Arrange the symbols on the quilt and shuffle them around to get the best layout. When you are satisfied with your design, stick the drawings onto the master sheet to produce your finished chart.

Pattern Library

In this Pattern Library you will find many more patterns, all designed for use on a 'mix and match' basis and to add to the basic patterns given elsewhere in the book. Choose the pattern you require, copy it out onto a separate piece of graph paper and incorporate it into your design. Small changes of detail will alter the patterns and make them more personal. People and their pets, cats and dogs, work, nationality, leisure, animals, sport, gardening, music, transport, signs of the zodiac, mottoes, borders and bands are all included here to help you make a comprehensive record of your life.

If the pattern you have chosen is facing in the wrong direction, hold a small hand-mirror beside it and copy out the mirror image to reverse the direction. All the patterns are in colour, but you can of course change the colours to suit your own taste.

Study Plate 39 and see how the patterns were taken from the Library and adapted to represent my own family. The embroidery frame was added to the basic female figure and her arms were re-drawn, to produce an embroideress. The figure of the business man was given a beard and his bowler hat was removed, whilst the addition of a copy of the *Financial Times* and the £ sign on his briefcase indicate that he is an economist. To produce a favourite pony the only change to the horse and rider was one of colour. The gymnast has been dressed in the colours of her gymnastics club. These changes were simple to make and have made the design uniquely personal to this family. Hopefully you will find many patterns that are relevant to your own life or perhaps you will recognise friends and be tempted to design and embroider a special gift for them.

Plate 39 'The Verso Family'

FAMILY

Basic figures are given here for a man, a woman, a boy, a girl and a baby. These figures appear throughout the book and can be changed to suit your needs by simply altering small details when you are copying them. Study the figures throughout and see how the changes have been made. Draw out the basic figure, erase those features you wish to change and copy in the new details (Fig 61). To make figures taller, add a few squares to the length of the legs or the torso, and to make them shorter, use fewer squares. In this way several children can be given differing heights to indicate their ages and place in the family. The grandmother and grandfather have been seated in armchairs; the cat on the lap and the spectacles are, of course, optional. If you would prefer these figures to be standing, copy out the basic adult figure and add white

hair, spectacles or whatever features are needed to make them recognisable. A wheelchair has been included for the disabled, or for the elderly and infirm.

Uniforms have been designed for a Brownie, a Girl Guide, a Cub and a Scout; minor details can be changed to suit any troop.

In the Pets section (Plate 40) both common and more exotic species have been catered for. Since cats and dogs are the most common pets, more examples of different types and poses are to be found on Plates 46 and 47. A budgerigar, a parrot, tropical fish, goldfish, a canary, rabbits, a white mouse, a guinea pig, a snake and a tortoise complete the line up. If you have a more unusual pet, make a tracing of it from a book and square it up as described in Chapter 2.

▽ *Plate 40*   *Plate 41* ▷

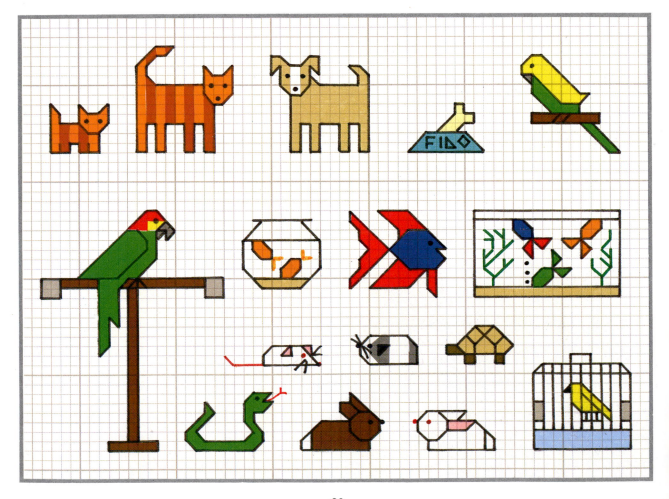

PEOPLE

As this book is about a personal approach to design, people appear regularly throughout, turning up in everything from greetings cards to full-scale samplers. The clothes that we wear can often indicate the work that we do, so one way of showing an occupation is to dress a figure appropriately. In some cases figures can also be shown using, or carrying, the tools of their trade.

Numerous examples of clothing, footwear and headgear are included in this section and many are interchangeable. To create a brand new figure, draw out the basic figure and add the hat of your choice, the hair style, clothing and shoes from other figures. With a little ingenuity you can create any uniform you need. The process of turning the hospital doctor figure into a family doctor is shown in Fig 61. Small changes of detail, such as the addition of a beard or spectacles, can make your figure even more closely resemble the real-life model.

The figures here are a chef (or maybe a baker), a painter or decorator, a fireman, a policewoman and a policeman (Plate 42). Next come a barrister, a civil engineer, a butcher, a teacher, a business man, a scientist, a traffic warden and a postman. The medical profession is represented by a doctor, a nurse, a surgeon and a dentist – note the dazzling smile (Plate 43).

The list continues with a pilot, a fisherman, a sailor, a soldier, an astronaut, a builder, a bride, a groom and a miner. The Church is represented by a bishop, a nun, a monk and a priest (Plate 44). Finally come a waitress, a cleaner, a beauty queen, a clown, a lacemaker, a barmaid, a hairdresser, an actor, a dancer and an artist (Plate 45).

▽ *Plate 42*

Plate 43 ▷ *(overleaf) Plates 44 and 45*

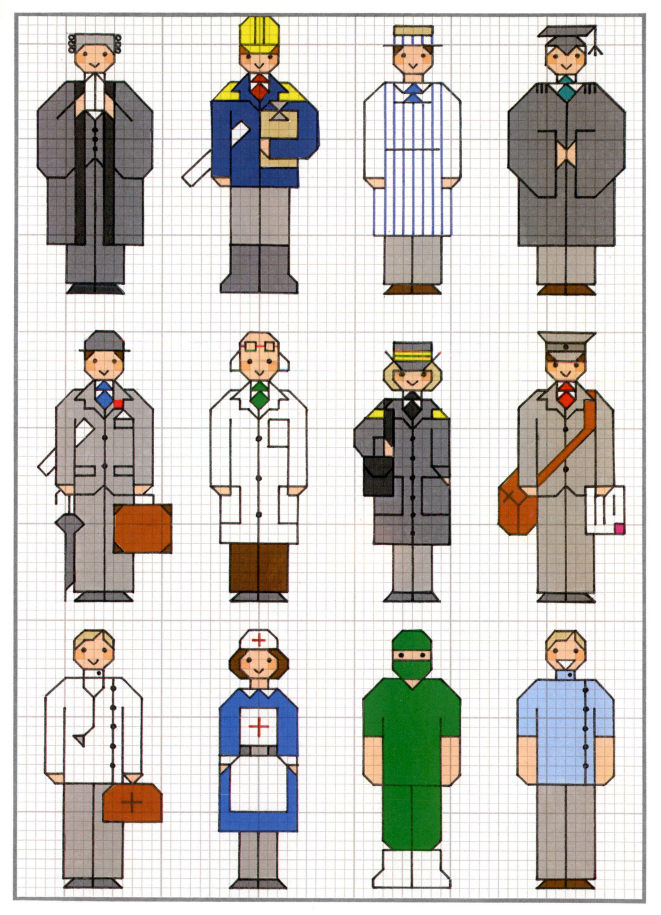

CATS AND DOGS

CATS (Plate 46)

Siamese cats are sewn with beige bodies and brown paws, ears and tails. Ginger cats can be striped with shades of soft orange, whilst tabbies get the same treatment with tones of grey. If you wish to record the fact that your cat is a good hunter, include a mouse or two. Long-haired cats are given a fuller body shape; study your animal and alter the colouring to suit its personal characteristics. Kittens and show cats have been included, together with a silver cup and rosette for glamour pusses.

DOGS (Plate 47)

It would take a whole book to include every breed of dog, but do not despair if your animal does not appear here. If you see a dog as a combination of a head shape, plus an ear shape, plus a body shape and a tail, many more breeds can be produced by mixing the material here. Experiment by putting different ears, tails or noses on different bodies. If this fails, visit your local library to get a picture of the breed and follow the tracing and squaring-up instructions in Chapter 2. You will have less awkward curves to deal with if you show the dog seated facing you, or you could try a lying down pose. If you place your dog in a kennel, you will only have the face to contend with. If all else fails, represent your dog by means of a feeding bowl showing its name.

Dogs in frames can represent pets which have died but which are still remembered with affection, or are useful where you do not have sufficient room to show the whole animal. Also they are ideal if the head is the only part you feel you have captured correctly, and the nether regions leave a lot to be desired.

▽ *Plate 46*   *Plate 47* ▷

OCCUPATIONS

If the occupation you wish to portray has no uniform or distinguishing clothing, you may be able to make use of the tools of the trade or the place of work. In this way the hammer and saw can represent a carpenter and the Stock Exchange can be used to represent a stockbroker. These pages have symbols for bankers, financiers and auditors (a magnifying glass has been placed over a £ sign), sales persons, computer operators, insurance brokers, business people, stockbrokers, typists, writers, telephonists and clerical workers (Plate 48).

Plate 49 has symbols to represent scientists, the medical profession, chemists, teachers, jewellers, weather forecasters, estate agents, photographers, film stars, politicians, the oil industry, garage owners, forecourt attendants, shopkeepers, shop assistants, film makers, draughtsmen, conjurers, locksmiths, security service personnel, electricians, geologists, factory

workers or owners, mechanics, home handymen, carpenters, heating engineers, plumbers, and anyone with a certificate showing his or her qualifications.

Allowing for all the possible meanings of these symbols, you could extend this list much further and include many more professions. Most of the symbols here have more than one meaning, and hence more than one use. For example, the typewriter could be used by a typist or by a writer; and the blackboard can indicate what is taught if the lettering on the board is changed to suit the subject. Computer operators, programmers, manufacturers, retailers and teachers of computer science can all make use of the pattern of a computer. If the occupation is in the leisure industry you may find what you want in the Home and Leisure or the Sport section. Even the Transport section can be of use, as the name of a firm or company can be back stitched onto the side of a van or a lorry.

▽ *Plate 48*   *Plate 49* ▷

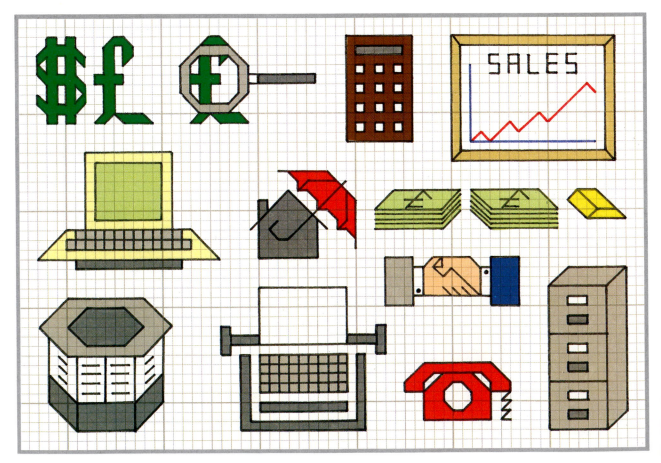

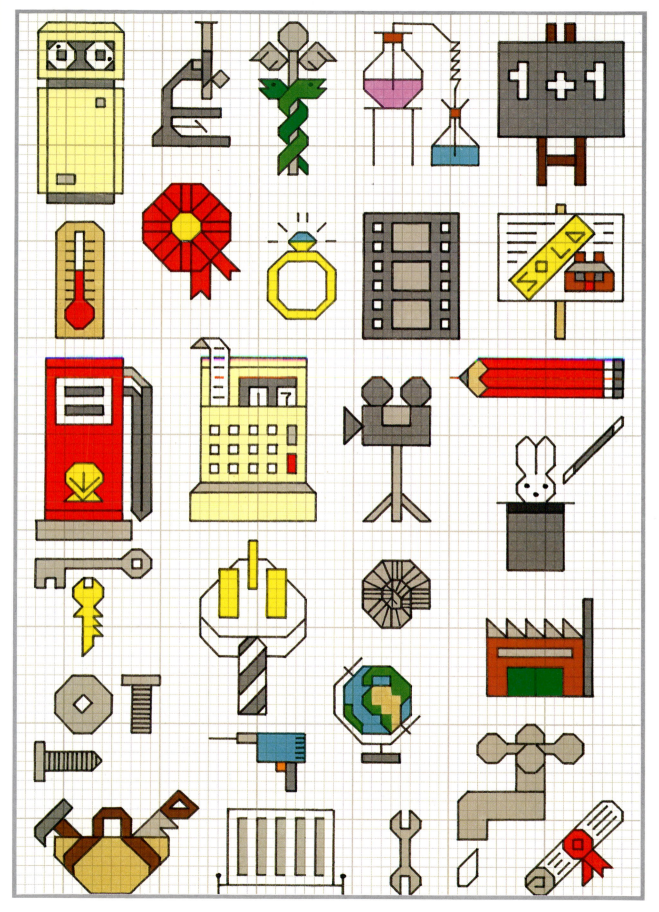

NATIONALITY

There are numerous ways to reflect nationality in your work, but perhaps the easiest way is to use a flag. Many flags are simple combinations of stripes, or consist of crosses, neither of which should present many difficulties in designing for cross stitch. The flag of the USA will require purists to sew fifty French knots onto the blue background after it has been stitched in full cross stitch, but as it stands here it is recognisable. The Union Jack can be reproduced fairly accurately, using three-quarter cross stitch for the diagonal stripes. The stars of the Southern Cross will need to be added in back stitch to the Australian flag when the blue background of full cross stitches has been worked.

National plants can be used: the English rose, the thistle of Scotland, the Welsh leek and the Irish shamrock can be found here in two sizes. Your choice of size will depend on the space you have available, or the promi-

nence you wish to give to the symbol. Native animals should not be overlooked, hence the koala. For the musically inclined, you may even consider using the National Anthem. The first few bars of 'God Save the Queen' have been drawn out here.

Costume associated with a country can be colourful and need not necessarily be the official national costume. Here the English morris dancer carries the handkerchiefs which he waves whilst dancing and wears the traditional hat decorated with flowers. The Scotsman is dressed in his kilt, which can be sewn to suit any clan; the background colours are worked first in full cross stitch, then back-stitch lines in a contrasting colour are worked over the top to give the effect of tartan. Examples of figures of other nationalities are included, all easy to identify.

The seven-branched candlestick, the *menorah*, can be used to represent Judaism.

▽ *Plate 50*   *Plate 51* ▷

108

HOME AND LEISURE

This page will help you to represent work in the home and leisure activities. What is leisure to some, will be work to others, so many of the symbols here will have a double meaning. Thus the suitcase can represent leisure to a holiday maker, or work to a travel agent. The fireplace is the heart of the home, or work for chimney sweeps and coal merchants. The ironing board represents sheer torture for me, but is a soothing pastime to others. For the kitchen you will find examples of appliances, crockery and food; vegetarians will find vegetables in the Gardening section.

The radio and television can represent either an interest in listening and viewing, or work in broadcasting, or even a repair business. A lace bobbin is included for lacemakers and bobbin makers. The piece of knitting in progress is back stitched after the cross stitch is completed, to show the rows, and the knitting pins are finished with two French knots. Dressmakers and tailors will find a sewing machine, tailor's dummy, spools of thread, and a thimble and scissors. Naturally, an embroidery frame had to be included in a book such as this.

Other leisure activities include camping (tent), photography (camera), painting (easel), flower arranging (vase), ballet (shoes), drama (masks), games (die), card games (ace), philately (stamps), poetry or sculpture (bust), reading (book), and a jigsaw piece for jigsaw addicts. The clock is for antique collectors or for clock repairers. The silver cup has been included for those who excel at their hobby and win prizes for it.

Do not overlook the organisation or club to which you may belong or for which you may work. Many organisations have badges suitable for squaring-up into cross-stitch patterns.

▽ *Plate 52*   *Plate 53* ▷

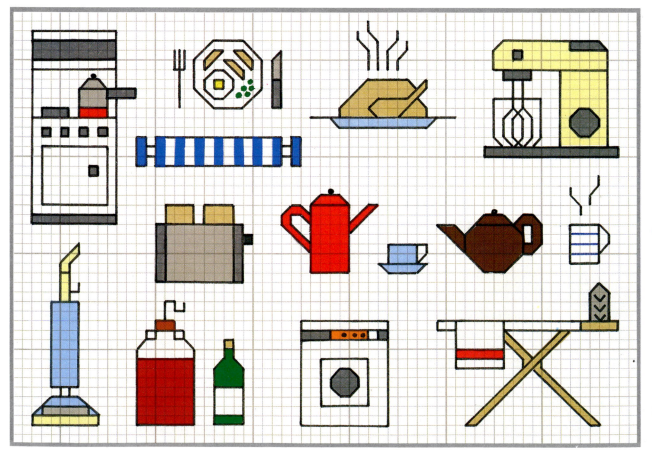

ANIMALS

Country dwellers, farmers, and those who work with animals or who have unusual pets may want to include in their designs the animals they see each day.

The bull has a ring in his nose which can be worked in gold thread. A Hereford bull, adapted from the pattern here, appears in Fig 62, so the shape and colour of both the cow and the bull can be altered to produce other breeds. Equally, many breeds of pig are possible if the colouring is changed. The sheep is accompanied by a ram, which is just a basic sheep shape with added horns. The horse has been given a saddle, which can be easily removed, and the donkey has the distinctive dark cross on its back. Birds include the hen with her chicks, a goose, a turkey, a duck and a drake, a duck with ducklings, a swan and an owl.

Animals, if repeated in lines, can be made into borders and bands. Suitable candidates for this treatment are the bees, the mice, the snails and the ducklings. The frog fits neatly into a corner. Remember to make your animals face inwards and, where you have a long line of them, split the line in two and make each half face the centre; otherwise they will look as if they are about to walk, hop, fly or swim out of the picture.

More exotic animals can be produced by the tracing and squaring-up method described in Chapter 2. So, if you are the proud owner of anything from an aardvark to a zebra, all is not lost if your pet does not appear here. A visit to your library, and in particular to the children's section, could be helpful. There you should be able to find a simplified line-drawing of the beast you require.

▽ Plate 54

Plate 55 ▷

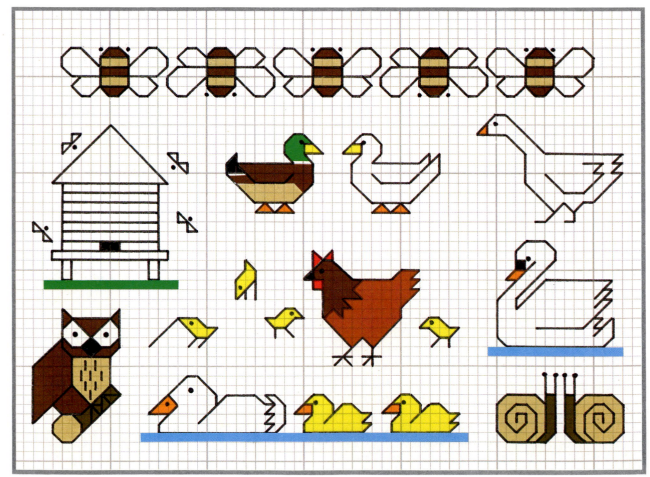

112

SPORT

Once again the basic figures have been drawn out and this time the appropriate sportswear has been added. The Coventry City football player holds the football and stands next to the FA Cup, but any team strip can be produced by changing colours. If you want a younger player, reduce the height by shortening the legs. Children invariably play with one sock up and one down, so adjust the socks accordingly. The referee has adopted a characteristic pose and has a whistle in his mouth.

Both male and female athletes are included and a medal can be placed around any neck or a figure can stand on a winner's rostrum for those who excel at their sport.

The golfer is in plus-fours to show off his socks, but he could be more casually dressed in golfing trousers and a peaked cap. Swimming is represented by the half-sub-merged swimmer doing the crawl and by the figure in a wet-suit with a snorkel. Jodhpurs, riding boots and a riding hat have been added to the basic girl figure to produce a rider, whereas the gymnast stands on her head and wears a leotard. If the sport you wish to represent has no special clothing to distinguish it, you may be able to make use of the equipment used in the sport, for example, the rifle to represent shooting.

When sewing strings onto tennis or squash racquets, use a darning technique with one strand of thread. Lay the horizontal threads between the cross stitches on the top of the work and weave the vertical threads in and out of the horizontal threads. At the end of one string bring the thread through to the back and out again at the beginning of the next string. The darning lies on top of the fabric and looks quite realistic.

▽ *Plate 56*   *Plate 57* ▷

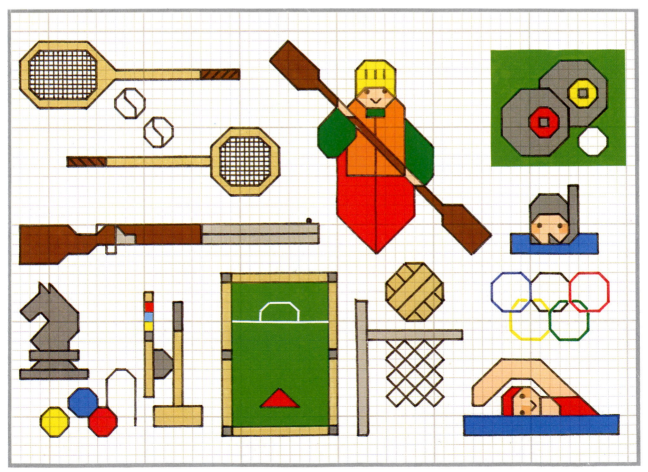

GARDENING

Throughout this book you will find many flowers and floral borders, any of which can denote a love of gardening. More flowers appear here as single specimens: poppy, violet, pansy, daisy, cornflower, fuchsia and general flower shapes, all of which can be used to create even more borders of the sewn rather than sown variety. Vegetables include asparagus, a leek, a carrot and a radish; fruit is represented by a strawberry, an apple and a pear. For a more energetic interest in gardening, include the wheelbarrow, watering-can, trowel, spade or hoe. The garden roller could represent the work of a groundsman.

Some garden furniture has been included: a table with a sun umbrella for those who prefer relaxing to working in the garden. Other garden features which can be useful when you are working on a design of your house are a window box, a hanging basket, a washing line, a sundial,

a rose arch and tubs of plants. The line of fencing can be extended to any length to form a band at the top or bottom of a design. A design for a complete garden picture appears in Plate 24. Whilst no two gardens are the same, you may be able to use a similar approach to immortalise your own plot.

For a sampler devoted to gardening, choose a border of flowers, butterflies or bees. Place the traditional alphabet and numbers at the top and choose a saying with a gardening theme to place at the bottom; Chapter 7 has many suggestions or you may have your own favourite. A gardener figure can be drawn by adding a gardening apron, gloves and watering-can to one of the basic figures. Fill the remaining space with any of the patterns in this section.

No garden is ever complete without a butterfly or two.

▽ *Plate 58*   *Plate 59* ▷

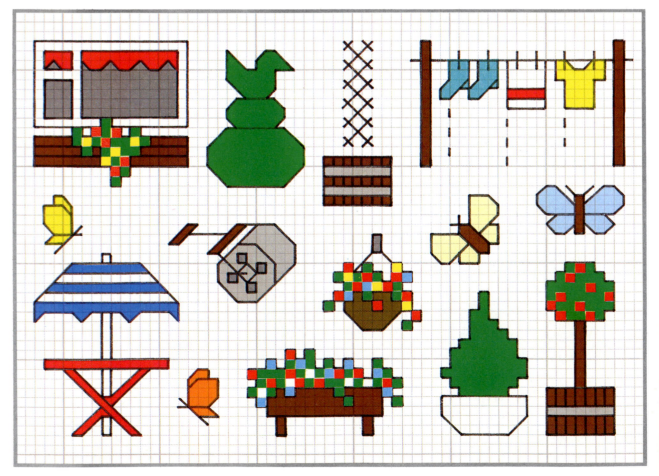

MUSIC

MUSICAL INSTRUMENTS

The instruments here are the piano, violin, 'cello, trumpet, trombone, tuba, French horn, saxophone, clarinet, drum, electric guitar, acoustic guitar, banjo and bagpipes. If sewing the bagpipes, choose your own tartan; embroider the basic squares and add the fine lines of colour over the top in back stitch. Strings, tuning pegs, keys, knobs and buttons can all be added in back stitch and French knots. The accordion, flute and recorder are shown with their players.

SINGING

Opera singing is represented by the performers. Brünnhilde and Carmen have been designed for you, but using the basic figure and a little ingenuity, any role is possible. For Madame Butterfly, turn to Plate 50.

A choir boy represents choral singing or church music, but an adult version can be produced using an adult basic figure as your starting point.

Gilbert and Sullivan lovers will recognise performers in the *Pirates of Penzance,* the *Yeomen of the Guard* and *The Gondoliers.* For performers in *The Mikado,* see Plate 50, and for *Trial by Jury,* see Plate 43.

MUSICAL NOTATION

Any bars of music can be drawn out quite accurately. Use back stitch to embroider the stave and whole crosses for the notes if you have room; if not, use French knots. Favourite tunes can be reproduced in their entirety if you have the patience, and can then be decorated with suitable designs and an appropriate border.

For a more general interest in music, use the record collection; the music stand is included for all conductors.

▽ *Plate 60*

Plate 61 ▷

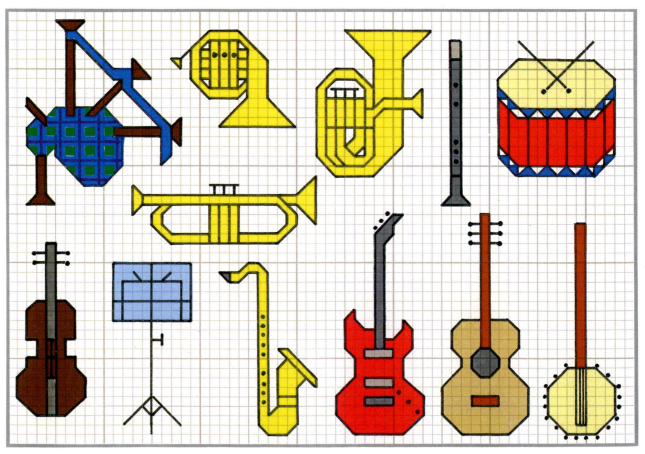

TRANSPORT

ROAD TRANSPORT

A general car shape is offered, which can be adapted to more closely resemble the make of car you want. More specialised are the taxi cab and the vintage car. Racing cars appear in two sizes, and if the small one is placed behind the large one, it is possible to achieve the effect of a race in progress. The design of a chequered black and white winning flag has been left for you to work out, which should not be too taxing, and will be appreciated by motor-racing enthusiasts. The bus has been designed face-on, a space-saving device which works well for many vehicles. A tractor has been included for farmers, a caravan for holiday makers, and a removal van for those on the move. The articulated lorry could have the name of a company written on the side, using back stitch. The push-bike can be adapted to a lady's model by removing the crossbar, and the drop handlebars can be replaced with upright ones. Two motor cycles complete this section.

SEAFARING

Sailing is represented by the small yacht and, on a much grander scale, the ocean-going liner. If you are going to design a large sailing ship, make liberal use of back stitch for all the rigging.

AIR TRAVEL

A modern jet is given in two sizes and a biplane for pioneering aviators. The hot air balloon can be enlarged to accommodate any pattern or wording you may wish to put on the fabric. A helicopter has also been included.

RAIL TRANSPORT

Two modern diesel locomotives can be found here and there are also two designs for steam buffs.

▽ *Plate 62*   *Plate 63* ▷

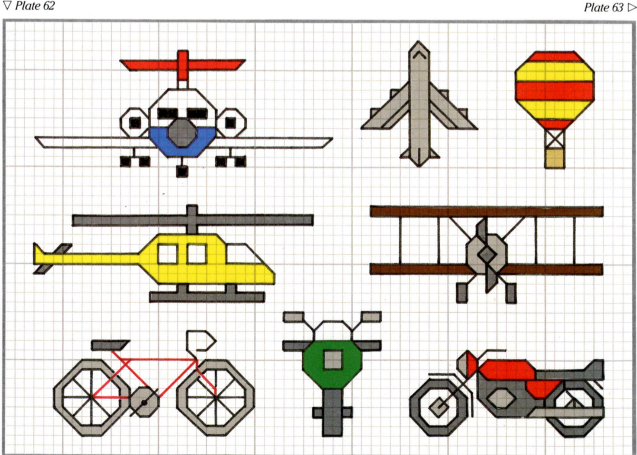

MOTTOES AND THE ZODIAC

Mottoes and sayings featured regularly and prominently on old samplers, where they tended to be of high moral tone and lugubrious nature. This was supposed to instruct the young needleworkers in the virtues of hard work, piety and filial obedience. For a contemporary style of work, use a modern quotation, or even something humorous. Whatever your choice of wording, mottoes can be written out in the alphabet of your choice and simply inserted into your design, or they can be illustrated.

Four examples are given here of mottoes accompanied by an illustrative symbol. 'Post tenebras lux', meaning 'After the darkness, light', is for optimists, the light being represented by a lamp. The text has been drawn onto a banner to give it extra emphasis. When drawing a banner for your text, try to get the same amount of text onto each of the end pieces, so that they are the same length.

The Girl Guide motto, 'Be Prepared', is placed above the Girl Guide badge. 'Make much of time' is written onto a banner and is illustrated by the obvious choice of a clock. 'Per ardua ad astra', the motto of the Royal Air Force, has two stars in the text.

You will have your own ideas; if not, *nil desperandum*.

PISCES	Feb 20 – Mar 20	VIRGO	Aug 24 – Sept 23
ARIES	Mar 21 – Apr 20	LIBRA	Sept 24 – Oct 23
TAURUS	Apr 21 – May 21	SCORPIO	Oct 24 – Nov 22
GEMINI	May 22 – Jun 21	SAGGITARIUS	Nov 23 – Dec 21
CANCER	Jun 22 – Jul 23	CAPRICORN	Dec 22 – Jan 20
LEO	Jul 24 – Aug 23	AQUARIUS	Jan 21 – Feb 19

Two sizes are given for each star sign. Depending on the prominence you wish to give the sign, or the space available, choose either the large pictorial version or the small symbolic one.

▽ *Plate 64* *Plate 65* ▷

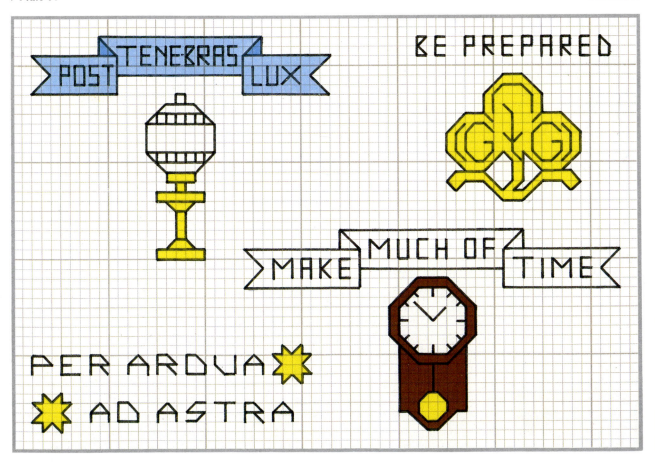

BANDS AND BORDERS

Here are more bands and borders for you to use. The bands (Plate 66) will need the addition of a corner to turn them into borders. Study the instructions in Chapter 2 and use a small hand mirror to help you to achieve this. To reproduce the apple blossom and butterfly border (Plate 23), two butterflies have been included; place them in the corners and at the reversal point in each strip of apple blossom. The borders can all be lengthened or shortened to fit your design; add extra pattern repeats to lengthen, or remove the necessary number of repeats to shorten, as the case may be.

Whatever border you choose or design, ask yourself if it would benefit from the addition of a retaining line. In some cases two lines on the outside and one on the inside can be effective (Plate 31). Experiment with coloured crayons and graph paper to make geometric borders if these are more to your taste. Plate 26 shows a simple geometric border which is easy to construct and can be made to any width desired.

Borders and bands have already been discussed in Chapter 2, where there are two more pages of ideas to choose from (Plates 4 and 5). Throughout the book you will find yet more borders surrounding designs; but if none of these is suitable there are many small designs which can be repeated to create the border you require. A student in one of my classes, who was a midwife, made a sampler border consisting solely of babies; another student, a keen stamp collector, did the same with rows of different coloured stamps. As well as being memorable, both were most effective and added a strong personal touch which is, after all, the whole object of the exercise and the constant theme of this book.

▽ *Plate 66* *Plate 67* ▷

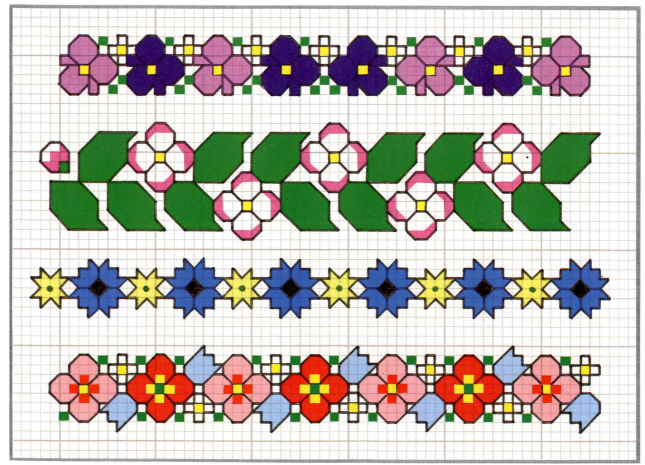

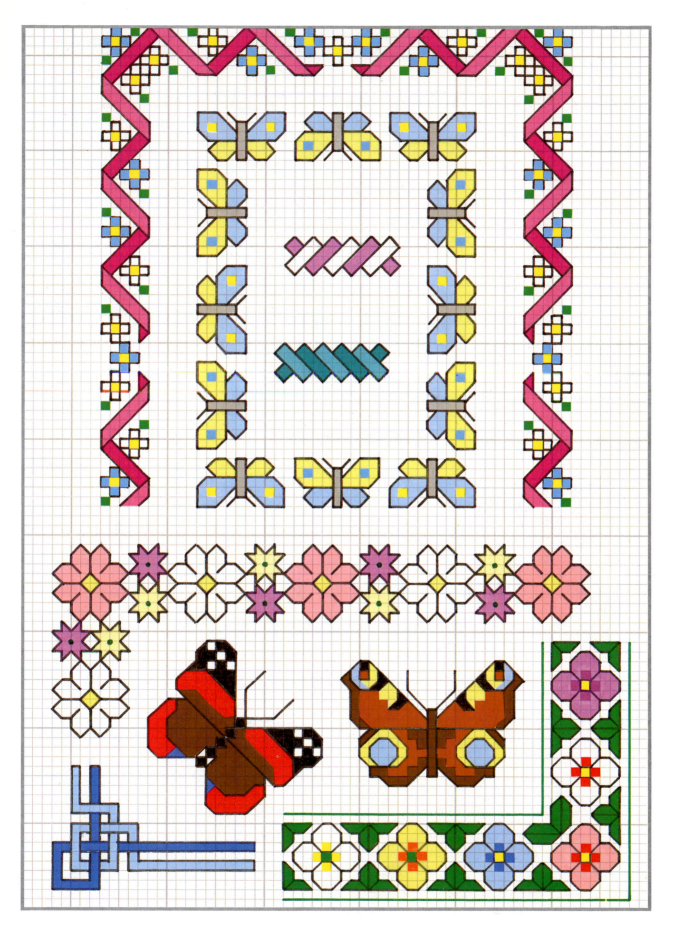

12 Finishing and Framing

When you think that your embroidery is complete, check it to make sure that you have worked everything on your pattern, and that you have not left any part of the design unworked other than the ground. Now is the time to sign and date your work, to claim it as your own and for the interest of future generations. Check that you have finished off all loose ends at the back of the work, as any stray threads lying behind unworked ground may show through when the work is mounted.

Your finished work should be clean if you have taken steps to protect it whilst work was in progress. If there has been some mishap, or the work needs freshening up, you may have to wash it before it is mounted. This is to be avoided if at all possible, and the following instructions are for newly completed work only. (If you are contemplating washing an old piece of work seek specialist advice before starting or the results could be disastrous.) If you are forced to wash your recently completed work, first test the threads for colour fastness. Modern threads are generally reliable, but it is better to be safe than sorry. Moisten a cotton bud in some tepid water and rub it over the back of the stitches. If no colour comes off on the cotton bud, it is probably safe to wash the piece.

Use tepid water, of the same temperature as the test you carried out, and thoroughly dissolve some good quality soap flakes in it. Whilst washing your embroidery avoid any pulling or rubbing, as this will distort your stitches; a gentle swish round should be sufficient to dislodge any grime. Rinse well using several changes of tepid water. Do not wring your work out as, again, this would distort the stitching. To dry, lay the work flat on a clean white towel and do wait until it is thoroughly dry. If work is framed behind glass, with any trace of moisture present, mould can cause severe problems later, producing unsightly stains on your work which will ruin it.

If you have kept your work rolled onto a tube for storage, as previously recommended, there should not be too many stubborn creases to remove. There is no need to block and stretch cross-stitch embroidery as in canvas work. If a hoop or a frame has been used, or where they have not, if a good, even tension has been maintained, a light press should be all the work needs to prepare it for mounting. To press your work there is no need to dampen it. Lay a thick, fluffy, white towel on a flat surface. Place your work face down onto the towel and cover it with a clean, white, cotton cloth. Press gently with a warm iron, nudging the iron up to the edges of the stitching, thus only pressing the unworked fabric. If you need to press the stitching itself, you can. The towel will allow the stitches to sink into its pile and the work will be pressed without flattening the stitches. Stitching which has been subjected to heavy pressing will look flat and lifeless. When pressed, your work is ready to be mounted.

If you do not wish to have your work framed, it can be mounted onto hardboard. The hardboard needs to be covered with a clean, cotton fabric to ensure that there is no contact between it and the work. Take care to choose a cotton fabric that is plain and of a colour which does not show through. Using a strong button thread or fine cord, the work is then laced in place on the back of the board from side to side and from top to bottom (Fig 71). The work will need to be removed from the board periodically for cleaning as it will not be protected by glass.

Hopefully, having spent so much time and effort on your design and the embroidering of it, you will think that your work deserves expert framing to give it the professional finishing touch. Most framers mount embroidery onto card, which is less bulky than hardboard. Check with your framer that the work will be mounted onto acid-free card. If the card is not acid-free, foxing can occur which produces unsightly brown patches after a while. Ask your framer not to allow the glass to come into contact with the stitches as this will flatten them. Use a mount made of acid-free card to raise the glass off the work, or ask the framer to raise the glass by means of thin strips of card packed around the edge of the frame where the overlap will hide them from view. Non reflective glass can be used, but my preference is for plain glass which gives a clearer view of the stitches.

Consider carefully where your 'masterpiece' is to hang. Avoid hanging it in direct sunlight which will fade the colours and rot the fabric eventually, but equally do not hide it away in the gloom where it will rarely be seen or admired.

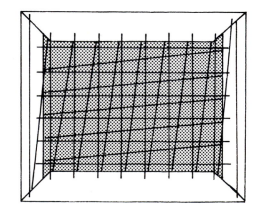

Fig 71 Lacing work onto hardboard

Acknowledgements

The author wishes to thank the following suppliers for their excellent service and assistance in the preparation of this book:

Stoneleigh Visual Services Centre, Leamington Spa (photographers of Plates 2, 3, 10, 21, 24, 26, 27 and 38)

Photography 2000, Newton Abbot (photographers of Plates 1, 6, 8, 12, 15, 17, 19, 22, 23, 25, 29, 30, 32, 33, 34, 36 and 37)

The Nimble Thimble, Rugby

Iris Woolcraft Centre, Leamington Spa

The Campden Needlecraft Centre, Chipping Campden (all suppliers of fabric, thread and general embroidery requirements)

J. & P. Coats (UK) Limited, Glasgow (suppliers of Anchor embroidery threads)

Dunlicraft Ltd, Leicester (suppliers of D.M.C. threads, Zweigart fabrics and greetings card mounts)

Wembley Graphics, Wembley (suppliers of graph paper and graphed tracing paper)

Warwick Studios, Warwick (framers)

Sources of design material

The author is indebted to the following publications which contain patterns which appear in photographs of her early work. All are recommended as valuable sources of inspiration and design material:

97 Needlepoint Alphabets by B. Borssuck (Arco, 1975) This was the source of the alphabet in Plate 27, and contains other alphabets of many sizes and styles.

1001 Designs for Needlepoint and Cross Stitch by the same author (Arco, 1977) contains many ideas for borders and bands.

Danish Cross Stitch Zodiac Samplers by Jana Hauschild (Dover, 1980). A book of charted designs for the astrological year, showing a design for each sign of the zodiac. Jana Hauschild has designed twelve magnificent floral borders reflecting the different seasons, together with alphabets and many other useful designs. The rose border, saxophone, butterfly, clover and garland (Plate 3) came from this source.

Arets Korssting 1982 by Ida Winckler (Haandarbejdets Fremme, 1982). Ida Winckler's Danish calendar contains many charming traditional patterns, amongst which are the love birds (Plates 2 and 3) and the garlands (Plate 38).

Leisure Arts leaflets:

No 49   *Charted Needlework Designs* (the egg whisk, Plate 3)

No 190   *Just for Baby* (the birds on the nest, Plate 38)

No 280   Keepsake Samplers (lettering, baskets of flowers, Plate 2: the border, Plate 38).

D.M.C. Point de Croix 6eme Serie (basket of flowers, Plate 38).

Graphique Needle Arts Book 15   *Borders, borders, borders* (border, hearts and flowers band, Plate 2).

The illuminated name 'AMY' (Plate 10) was inspired by designs produced by Eva Rosenstand and Clara Waever who specialise in fine cross-stitch kits.

Further Reading

Colby, Averil. *Samplers* (Batsford, 1964)

Don, Sarah. *Traditional Samplers* (David & Charles, 1986)

Lammer, Jutta. *Making Samplers* (Sterling Publishing Co Inc, 1984)

Lewis, Felicity. *Needlepoint Samplers* (Cassell, 1981)

Meulenbelt-Nieuwburg, Alberta. *Embroidery Motifs from Dutch Samplers* (Batsford, 1974)

Sebba, Anne. *Samplers* (Weidenfeld & Nicolson, 1979)

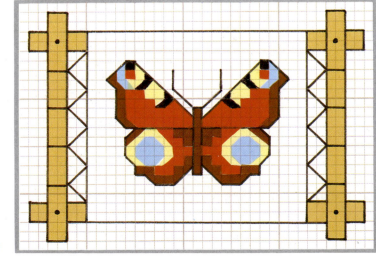

Plate 68

Index

Page numbers in italics indicate illustrations